Mastering QuickBooks

A Comprehensive Guide for Beginners to Streamlining

Financial Management and Bookkeeping

Kelvin Shelby

this book are for clarifying purposes only and are owned by the owners themselves, not affiliated with this document.

Table of Contents

Chapter One Introduction..1

Why QuickBooks..9

Understanding Accounting Basics 11

Basic Accounting Principles 13

Double Entry Accounting 16

Chapter Two Getting Started with QuickBooks 19

Features of QuickBooks...19

QuickBooks Online vs. QuickBooks Desktop..................22

Installing QuickBooks Software 23

Setting up a new company file..29

Navigating QuickBooks Interface.....................................32

Customizing QuickBooks Preferences..............................36

Chapter Three Chart of Accounts and Lists......................40

Creating and Managing Chart of Accounts.......................40

Adding an account 40

Edit an account..42

Delete an account..42

Inactivate an account. 42

Add account numbers...43

Working with Customers and Jobs 43

Managing Vendors and Suppliers 46

Setting up products and Services 48

Chapter Four Entering Transactions 52

Recording sales and invoices 52

Managing Expenses and Purchase Orders 55

Handling Banks and Credit Card Transactions 57

Enter Payroll Information 60

Reconciling and Reporting 61

Reconciling Bank and Credit Card Accounts 61

Generating Financial Statements 63

Customizing Reports for Business Analysis 64

Budgeting and Forecasting in QuickBooks 66

Chapter Five Payroll and Taxes 67

Setting Up Payroll in QuickBooks 67

Processing Employee Payroll and Taxes 68

Managing Payroll Liabilities 69

Handling Sales Tax in QuickBooks 71

Chapter Six Customizing QuickBooks for Specific Industries 73

QuickBooks for Retail Businesses 73

Tips for Retailers 74

QuickBooks for Service-based Companies 75

QuickBooks for Nonprofits and Charities................................... 76

QuickBooks for Construction and Contracting Businesses 77

Chapter Seven Advanced Features....................................... 80

Managing Inventory and Assemblies.................................... 80

Tracking Time and Mileage 81

Handling Multicurrency Transactions................................... 82

Using QuickBooks Add-ons and Integrations 84

Chapter Eight Troubleshooting and Tips 86

Common Errors and How to Fix Them 86

Optimizing QuickBooks Performance 87

Data Backup and Recovery Strategies 88

Tips and Tricks for Efficient Bookkeeping................................ 89

Chapter Nine Expanding Your Knowledge 92

Advanced Training Resources 93

Certified QuickBooks ProAdvisor Program 95

Online Communities and Forums for QuickBooks Users 96

Conclusion 98

Glossary of QuickBooks Terms.. 98

Keyboard Shortcuts Reference.. 99

Sample Forms and Templates 100

An Introduction to QuickBooks

In the ever-evolving business landscape, efficient financial management is necessary and the key to success. QuickBooks stands tall as the go-to solution for businesses of all sizes, offering a robust platform to simplify accounting processes and empower decision-makers.

Welcome to "Mastering QuickBooks," your indispensable guide to navigating this powerful accounting software's latest features and functionalities. Whether you're a seasoned entrepreneur, a small business owner, or an aspiring financial professional, this book is crafted to provide you with the knowledge and skills needed to harness the full potential of QuickBooks in the dynamic world of finance.

As technology continues shaping how we do business, staying ahead of the curve is crucial. This book not only walks you through the fundamentals but also delves into advanced techniques, tips, and strategies to optimize your financial workflows. Each chapter is designed to equip you with practical insights and hands-on expertise, from setting up your company file to mastering payroll, tracking expenses, and generating insightful reports.

Join us on a journey through the intricacies of QuickBooks, where we demystify complex accounting processes, tackle common challenges, and unveil the latest updates. Whether you're a solo entrepreneur managing your startup's finances or a financial professional overseeing a corporation's accounts, this book is your roadmap to achieving financial mastery through QuickBooks.

Get ready to unlock the full potential of QuickBooks and revolutionize how you manage your finances. Let's embark on this journey together, where efficiency meets innovation, and financial success becomes more than just a goal – it becomes a reality.

Chapter One

Introduction

It is 2023, and at the core of the bookkeeping and finance management processes of almost every small or medium-sized business is QuickBooks. QuickBooks is an intuitive, user-friendly bookkeeping and accounting software developed by Intuit Company that is equipped with extensive capacity and tools to perform just about any conceivable bookkeeping or accounting task required for a business's financial management and health. Among these, numerous tasks include regular valuable accounting tasks such as bookkeeping, taking inventory, generating and sending invoices, payroll administration and management, expense control, budgeting, making and processing payments, time and bank account tracking, and managing account receivables and payable. As much as QuickBooks is very valuable to businesses, it is also useful to personal individuals who are self-employed or individuals who want to keep a record of their finances. With QuickBooks, businesses or self-standing freelancers can automate these accounting processes, making financial tracking and management easier and faster. Once an individual's or a business's finances are, one can focus on profitable strategies to improve finances or other aspects of the business or individual's life. Quickbooks can be purchased and used on mobile phones and computers. There are different versions of QuickBooks, which are usually compatible with most devices.

Nevertheless, it is important to be sure that the version to be installed and bought on a device is compatible with the device and its operating system. QuickBooks for Mac is the QuickBooks software built for Macbooks and MacOS, while QuickBooks Desktop is the version of QuickBooks built to work for the Windows operating system. QuickBooks for Mac can be purchased at a fixed price. It is designed with features for the optimal use of QuickBooks with MacOS. QuickBooks Desktop for Windows has different versions and packages, including QuickBooks Pro, QuickBooks Premier, QuickBooks Enterprise, and QuickBooks Accountant. The purchase price of the packages increases as the versions and features are upgraded. You can download and install QuickBooks Desktop on your desktop and go ahead and buy the QuickBooks Desktop package of your choice. You can also access the Payroll feature by buying any additional Payroll plans. There are no monthly subscriptions for QuickBooks Desktop. Purchase and subscription for the Quickbooks Desktop versions (and other additional plans) usually lasts for a year. Another type of QuickBooks is the QuickBooks Online. QuickBooks Online is a cheap, flexible, and convenient version of QuickBooks that also possesses excellent accounting tools. This version is an internet cloud-based version. It can be accessed by anyone connected to the internet on any device (including mobile phones). Data input goes directly to the Intuit cloud storage, which is safe, secure, and accessible on any device once you sign in to the account online. However, features and services on QuickBooks Online are somewhat limited. Hence, you must pay additional prices or subscribe to QuickBooks Online plans to unlock and use upgraded features.

In order of ascending price and features, the QuickBooks plans include the "Self Employed" plan for freelancers and sole businesses as the name implies, the "Simple Start" also for individuals, solo businesses, and startup companies, the "Essentials" plan which is suitable for a growing business that can now has up to three employee (or users) that can be added to the QuickBooks account, the "Plus" plan which allows up to five users to software, and finally the "Advanced" plan that offers the most accounting feature and allows more than five people access the application. The pricing for QuickBooks Online can be monthly or yearly. Other Intuit software can be integrated with QuickBooks Online and QuickBooks Desktop, such as ProConnect (a tax software for accounting professionals), TurboTax (software for setting up personal income tax), or other software designed by other companies. The QuickBooks Multicurrency feature is an outstanding feature of QuickBooks Online that allows multinational businesses to manage their account in the different currencies they deal with. This feature is available with Plus, Essentials, and Advanced plans.

QuickBooks is an easy-to-use program. The general user interface of QuickBooks consists of the Home page, Icon bar, and Menu bar. The Home page is the default display on the large screen when QuickBooks is opened, while the Menu bar is located at the top of the screen, and the Icon bar is at the left corner of the screen. However, the QuickBooks Desktop interface is different from the QuickBooks

Online interface, and the features available in the Menu and Icon bars depend on the version or plan in use.

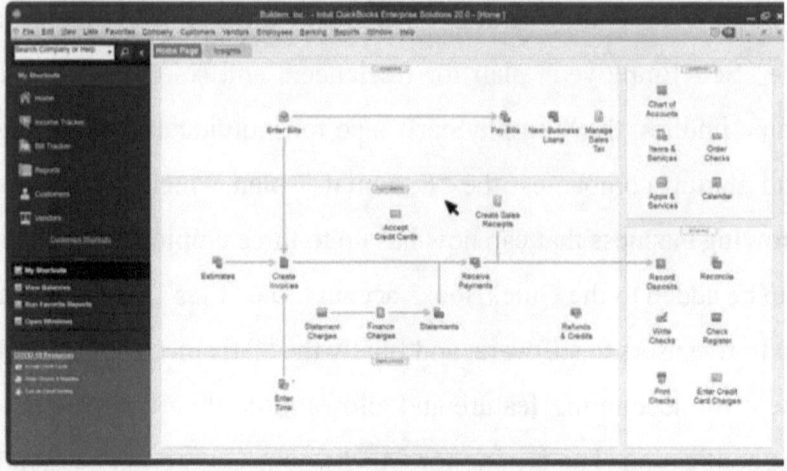

Figure showing QuickBooks Desktop interface

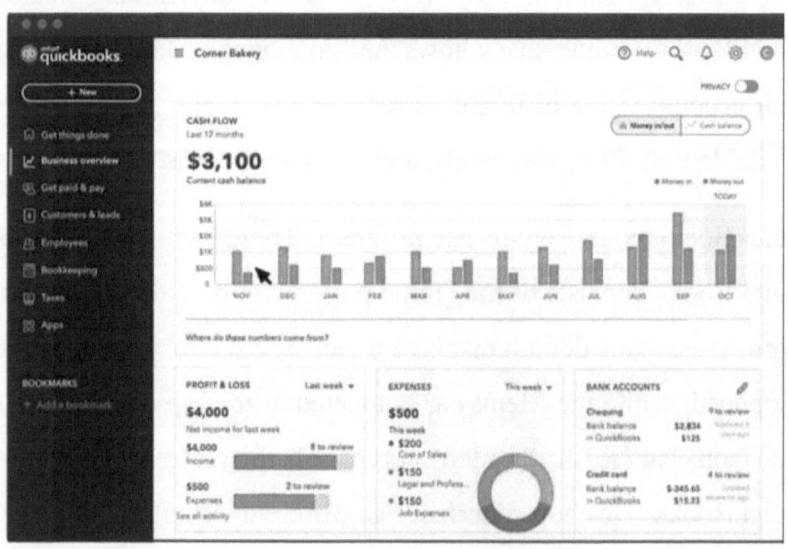

QuickBooks Online interface

QuickBooks Online has two views - A "business view" designed for people running a business but with no accounting background and a typical "accountant view" for professional accountants and individuals with accounting knowledge. The accounting features in the Menu and Icon bar change as the view changes. You can switch between views by selecting "Switch to Business View" and "Switch to Accountant view" at the bottom right corner in the "Settings" menu.

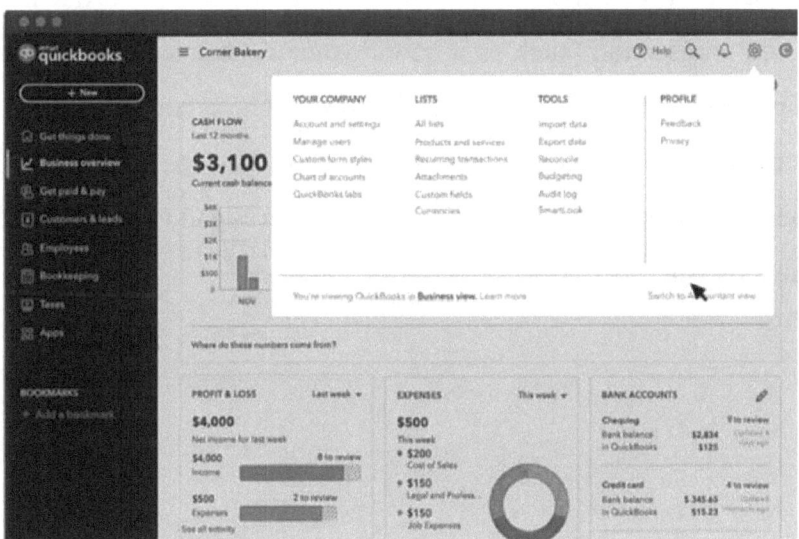

Switching between QuickBooks Online views

The QuickBooks Online Menu bar is located at the top right corner of the screen. It consists of the symbols for "help," "settings," "search," "notifications," and "profile" menus. In "settings," you can change and optimize the settings of QuickBooks to suit your preferences. The Icon bar consists of icons for carrying out transactions and account management, such as "+ New," "Get things done," "Business Overview," "Get paid and pay," "Apps," and "Bookkeeping. " "Get things done" is a shortcut to commonly used features such as creating invoices, paying bills, adding customers, and accessing reports. "Business overview" includes cash flow, reports, and projects. In the "Apps" section, you can connect other applications such as "Etsy," "Square," "ProConnect," and "MailChimp." When you need to perform a new transaction (such as a new invoice or expense) for customers, suppliers, or employees, select "+ New." The other icons have their purposes, and the icon's name can easily be known. In the accountant view of QuickBooks, more accounting features and tools are present in the Icon bar.

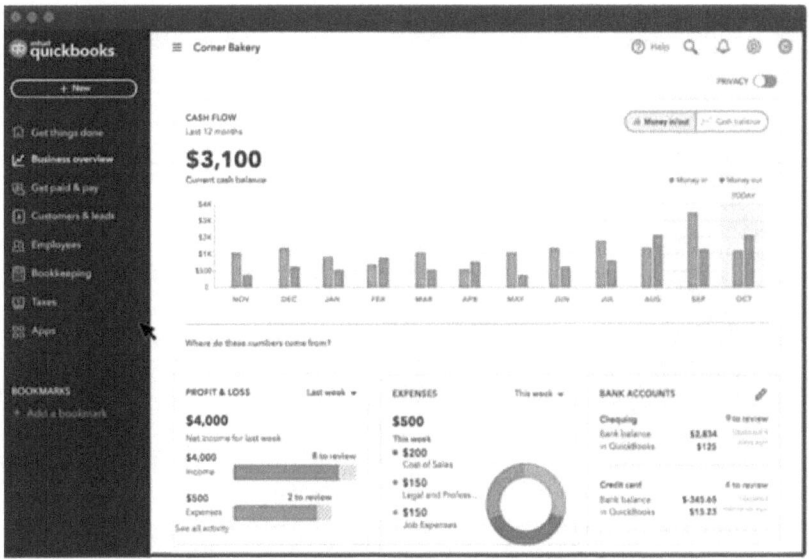

QuickBooks Online interface showing Home page, Icon bar, and Menu bar

In QuickBooks Desktop, the default Home page displays routinely used accounting tools in charts and workflows that tell you how to run your business transactions. The Menu bar is located across the top left of the screen, containing different menus such as File, Edit, View, List, Favorite, and Company. These menus usually contain more tasks compared to the Home page tasks. The Icon bar is also located at the left side of the Home page, and it contains icons like "My shortcuts" (where you can add commonly used features), "New" (to begin new tasks), "View Balances, "Run favorite reports, "Open Windows to navigate and use tasks.

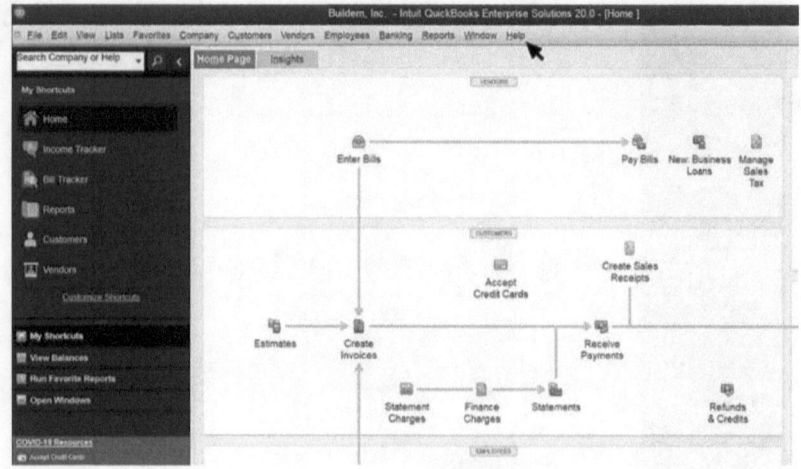

QuickBooks Desktop Home page, Menu bar, and Icon bar.

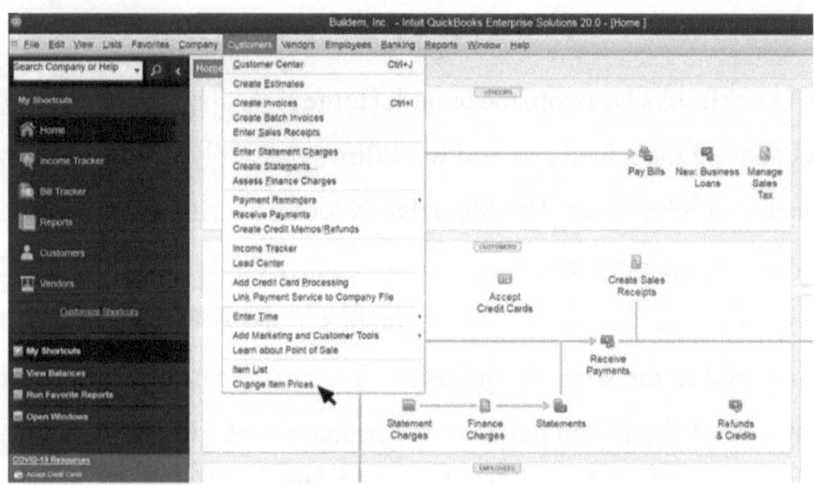

More commands are seen in the Menu bar.

Why QuickBooks

If you own a business, you can discover that you may have to take on different tasks outside your managerial role. Some tasks include payroll, accounting, and preparing for tax season. Carrying out these bookkeeping tasks or hiring and paying an accounting firm to take on the roles can be time-consuming. Here, we talk about the reasons you should use QuickBooks.

Flexibility

QuickBooks is one of the accounting software that gives its users flexibility. The QuickBooks Online plan allows small businesses to achieve administrative tasks like creating invoices. Users can use QuickBooks online from a smartphone, PC, or MAC. QuickBooks also displays flexibility by making it easy to sync many files in real-time and work on them simultaneously. You can also sync their data from popular apps like Tsheets and Square.

Filing Taxes

If you still have a container filled with transaction details and receipts, you can make filing taxes hard for your accountant. He spends hours or days getting the relevant information, and still, there is a likelihood of a mistake. All the data is kept in a place and can be easily accessed when needed using QuickBooks. In addition, each transaction detail and bank statement is there for your accountant to see and confirm, making the tax filing process precise and easy.

Easily generate financial reports and invoice templates.

Using QuickBooks to create financial reports and invoices makes reporting, downloading, and sharing easy. You can also use different invoices and report templates. QuickBooks makes it easy to make financial reports by letting users make yearly income reports and financial forecast reports with an easy click. The reports can be sent to Excel for keeping records or sharing through email or print. These financial reports are good for little businesses as they are always trying to grow. The reports can help them note gaps in customer service, boost sales, document trends, and tailor a new marketing strategy to customers.

Easier money and inventory management

QuickBooks accounting software promotes the ease at which little business owners can keep tabs on their revenue, expenses, and payroll information for employers. With QuickBooks, you can record bill due dates and type payment information for bills. Small business owners can link their ban accounts easily to QuickBooks, allowing them to look at their financial records simultaneously. In dah to say operations, small business owners accumulate various expenses. You can easily track the buying and selling of inventory. As you change an inventory for a client,

QuickBooks updates the information so small businesses know the accurate inventory and the quantity.

It ascertains the timely payment.

The essence of keeping financial reports, records, and invoices is to get paid quickly. Software with beautiful features without delivering the benefits it created to its users is useless. With QuickBooks, you can make invoices, send them to clients, and confirm whether they have seen the invoice.

It saves time

QuickBooks makes the bookkeeping process easy. Single tasks like downloading transactions and signing checks can be completely automated. For instance, you can save the signature in the system to sign someone's checks.

Understanding Accounting Basics

Importance of Accurate Accounting

Although not the most thrilling part of a business, accounting is unarguably important. At the heart of any business, money (funds) is coming in and going out, and it is wise to have a correct and up-to-date record of these financial transactions. An accurate financial record is critical for any organization, whether big or small. Amongst other advantages, authentic records help businesses stay productive and well-organized and make rational choices. Accurate and consistent accounting provides a detailed view of the financial health of a company, especially its revenue, and expenses, making it easier for business owners and managers to track records, assess the company's growth and development chain, and essentially identify areas where they could cut cost or increase income. In addition, accurate accounting records aid businesses in executing better inventory and cash flow management. It ensures that businesses have enough cash to pay all their bills (e.g., suppliers and taxes) and prevents them from falling short of goods and services. Maintaining proper record-keeping is also necessary to ensure compliance with government tax regulations. It allows businesses to pay their correct taxes on time to avoid legal penalties, as inaccurate tax fillings due to improper records by the organization may result in costly fines and even confinement. Consistent and reliable accounts also serve as a premise to cultivate trust with customers and important stakeholders and apply for and eventually receive more funds from these stakeholders and other organizations like the banks.

With consistent and reliable records, a business can mitigate potential dangers and losses (from creditors). Accurate accounting is not just about having current financial statements, debits, and credits; it is also essential for human resources management, such as payroll sheets. If an organization does not have a suitable system for keeping records of these transactions could face serious financial complications like excess cost, funds mismanagement, and even legal issues.

Basic Accounting Principles

Accounting principles are the generally accepted standards and rules that are to be adhered to by businesses and other organizations when recording and reporting financial transactions. These accounting principles give a degree of generalized structure to financial accounts and statements, making them easy to comprehend and review. The concept of these basic principles for accounting was established through the widespread use of these rules. The International Financial Reporting Standards (IFRS) represent the most extensively utilized collection of accounting guidelines. Some other jurisdictions adopt a distinct set of accounting principles to follow. Generally Accepted Accounting Principles (GAAP) are used in the United States. These basic accounting principles are set by accounting bodies of a region and are put in place to enhance the quality of a business's accounting records to make them complete, consistent, and comparable. Without these, the records cannot be maximally used to understand the financial status of a business. The most recognized basic principles include the following;

- **The Conservatism principle** states that liabilities and costs should be acknowledged and recorded as soon as feasible, even if they are uncertain, but the recording of assets and income should be delayed until they are assured. This results in a more cautious record of profit and loss, often favoring the recording of losses as soon as possible rather than later.
- **Accrual Principle**: this rule suggests that accounting transactions should be recorded in periods when they happen rather than when

there is related cash flow. The accrual basis of accounting is based on this. For instance, disregarding the accrual basis would be to record an expense only after its payment.

- **Consistency Principle**: rule that once you use a particular accounting principle, you should stick to it until a superior one is discovered. Adherence to this principle produces a structured financial record that is easy to review.

- **Reliability Principle**: the rule that only transactions that can be proved with physical evidence (such as purchase receipts, canceled checks, and bank statements) should be documented in the accounting system of a business. A third party usually provides this evidence as they would be more believable.

- **The Period principle** states that there should be a standard period in which financial outcomes can be reported. It could be monthly, quarterly, or annually. Consistency in reporting at the selected standard period is important to produce comparable financial statements.

- **The Cost Principle** states that an asset, liability, or share must be recorded in its original purchase cost. This Principle is adopted because it is simple to use the original purchase cost as objective and reliable proof of worth. However, since fair value is becoming increasingly prevalent in accounting rules, t his principle is becoming less applicable.

- **The Matching principle** mandates that every cost associated with a transaction that generates revenue should be recorded while the income is recognized and recorded. Accrual accounting is based on this principle since related revenue and expenses are recorded within the same reporting time.

- **The Materiality Principle** recommends that transactions that might impact a user's (or accountant's) decision-making should be included in the financial statements. According to generally accepted accounting principles (GAAP), immaterial transactions do not have to be recorded, making this principle quite unclear to a majority of inexperienced individuals who may be unable to distinguish immaterial transactions.

- **The Economic Entity Principle** states that each business entity's recorded account and bank transactions should be kept apart from those of its owner or owners and other business entities. It means you have to attribute every business transaction to an entity. The concept of this principle keeps the financial outcomes of different entities from getting mixed up.

- **The Full Disclosure Principle** is the idea that everything that could affect a reader's comprehension of a company's financial statements should be included or provided alongside them. As a result, many financial statements now come with a sizeable amount of footnote disclosure.

- **Going concern principle**. This principle allows for postponing the recognition of certain expenses until later due to the presumption that the business will continue to operate in the foreseeable future. Because of this principle, companies do not have to sell their assets, but it can keep them to a time when they can be used maximally.

- **The Monetary Unit or Currency Principle** states that only business transactions with monetary value or currency should be recorded. As a result, non-quantifiable possessions such as the business quality control value, staff skill levels, and customer service standards cannot be recorded. This principle prevents an organization from overestimating when determining the worth of its assets and liabilities.

- **The Revenue Recognition Principle** implies that revenue should be recognized after the business has effectively finished all the processes towards the earning, even if the payment has not been made. This principle is also based on accrual accounting. Multiple principle-setting agencies have released information regarding the appropriate recognition of revenue due to the numerous individuals who have committed reporting fraud by bypassing this principle.

Double Entry Accounting

The double-entry system is one of the most vital bookkeeping and accounting elements. It is a bookkeeping method that forms one of the basics of accounting. In accounting, business transactions are documented in credits and debits into various business accounts (e.g. Assets, Liability, Expenses, Equity, Revenue, Gains, and Losses).

Double-entry accounting simply requires that every monetary transaction has an equal and opposing effect in at least two separate accounts. For each entry into one account, there is an equal and opposite entry made into a separate account. It means that while one or more accounts have a debit entry, some other one or more accounts have a similar credit entry. The origin of the double-entry system traces back thousands of years ago, when the Romans and the early Middle Eastern civilizations employed primitive versions of the system. The double-entry bookkeeping system has been in use since those times and has played an important role in business accounting, ergo the society. The wide use of the current Double-entry system started with Italian merchants in the 13th and 14th centuries. In 1494, Luca Pacioli, "Father of Accounting," wrote the first known publication on the principle of the double-entry system. The book outlined the details of the system.

The double-entry accounting system contradicts the single-entry accounting in which business transactions are recorded in only one account. For example, in double-entry, if an organization purchases office furniture worth $50,000 on credit, the asset (furniture) account will have a debit entry of $50,000 to account for the cost of the increased asset, while the liability account will have a credit entry of $50,000 to account for equipment bought on credit. If the purchase was made with cash, the asset (furniture) account will still be debited due to increased assets, while the cash account is credited for a decrease in cash. In the double-entry system, since a debit entry in one account results in a corresponding credit entry in another, all the debits must equal all the credits in the complete financial record.

Double-entry accounting provides a more balanced, broad, comprehensive, and transparent picture of every financial transaction and the organization's balance sheet. The method is based on the accounting equation "Assets = liabilities + Equity." It justifies this equation as it shows a balance in the company's financial record, equally showing its gains and losses or its assets and liabilities. The double-entry balance sheet is typically displayed in a "T-account," which allows a debit entry on the left side of the account and a credit entry on the right side. One side of the balance sheet shows all the increases, while the other entry shows all the decreases. A debit entry does not always indicate an increase, and a credit entry does not always indicate a decrease. It is, therefore, to know the accounts debited when there is an increase and credited when there is a decrease, and those debited for a decrease and credited for an increase. The former includes accounts such as Assets, Expenses, and Dividends, while the latter includes Liabilities, Revenues and gains, Retained earnings, and capital stock. For example, a debit to assets reflects an increase, while a credit to Liability reflects an increase.

Cash		Salary Payable		Revenue		Rent Expense	
Debit	Credit	Debit	Credit	Debit	Credit	Debit	Credit

Figure of "T-account"

Chapter Two

Getting Started with QuickBooks

Features of QuickBooks

➢ **Invoicing**

Make customized, professional invoices you would love and move from sent to paid in days. You can manage your money online and in a place and get paid fast. You can make quotes involving discounts, payments, and much more. You can easily do that by turning on your estimate to an invoice in one Click.

➢ **Track payments in Real-Time.**

See if an invoice is viewed, outstanding, or paid. Confirm the status of any invoice on your tablet, smartphone, and computer. QuickBooks displays your due or overdue invoices and sends personalized reminders to customers who pay late. You can also automate the invoice to create accurate invoices and save time when you do it.

QuickBooks automated invoicing software lets you set up automatic payment schedules for frequent clients. Send your invoices in batches or individually.

➢ **Taxes, discounts, and shipping**

Make invoices with tax and shipping costs discounted for you. QuickBooks keeps track of the amount you earn and owe.

➢ **Expenses**

You can easily track your business expenses in one place from your devices. You can automatically import and place your expenses in categories. Edit or approve the categorization or make custom rules you can follow. You can easily classify your transactions in bulk if need be.

> **Take expenses in an instant.**

Use your QuickBooks mobile to take pictures of your receipts anyplace, so you can save the attached to make transactions ahead of tax time.

> **Inventory**

Inventory tracking can be time-consuming for various small and medium-sized businesses. QuickBooks helps you manage the stock so you know what you have and need before you need them. You will also know what you have in your stock and what you need to buy. As you keep updating the new stocks, QuickBooks inventory manages your inventory, making it easy to see the items you sell out and what you should order. In addition, the inventory automatically calculates the cost of individual products sold with the help of first-in, first-out (FIFO).

> **Insight and reports.**

You can access the financial statements and reports instantly. You can easily see all the things you need for the business. You can also see a

360° view of your sales and filter out your data by product, customer, location, or project. You can access up-to-date financial reports, balance sheets, profit and loss statements, cash flow statements, and customized reports. For example, you can create a profit and loss statement. The statement is also an Income statement, providing detailed information on whether your business is operating at a loss or a profit. QuickBooks Online makes it simple to check the profit and loss statements in a few clicks, making it easy to evaluate where you can lower expenses, increase profit, and grow revenue.

> **Business reports are made easy.**

Vivid financial reporting leads to good business decisions. Look for real-time small business insights with financial statements like balance sheets, income statements, and cash flow statements on the QuickBooks dashboard. In addition, you can track payable tax and cash inflows and outflows. You can customize the report or your business based on your preference.

QuickBooks Online vs. QuickBooks Desktop

QuickBooks has two products: the QuickBooks online and the QuickBooks desktop. Here, we compare the benefits of the two offers, and then you can decide which one to use.

❖ QuickBooks Online is the best choice to enjoy robust features and a user-friendly interface. The QuickBooks desktop is a wonderful option for businesses that prefer desktop software to QuickBooks online because of its higher level of inventory tracking and reporting tools.

❖ QuickBooks is easy to use. You can invoice customers. It is a good invoicing software as it can calculate sales tax spontaneously to apply to an invoice based on your customer's address. It also combines third-party payment, making it easy for customers to pay their invoices online. QuickBooks desktop makes managing your books from many companies easy, provided you don't need a consolidated financial statement.

❖ QuickBooks allows you to access QuickBooks online from your computer and even mobile devices, provided it is connected to the internet. With this option, you can share your date with an accountant. QuickBooks is good for businesses that need to do intensive inventory accounting. QuickBooks online and desktop provide inventory accounting, but the QuickBooks desktop has in-depth inventory management tools. For example, manufacturing companies can use it to monitor their products using inventory assemblies and parts.

❖ QuickBooks Online smoothly combines different e-commerce platforms and provides a good inventory management feature, making it one of the best e-commerce accounting software. In addition, the QuickBooks desktop is good for you if you prefer to access your accounting program without an internet connection.

If you want to provide, allow two or more people to access your books, for instance, tax professionals. You should use QuickBooks online. If you want to use QuickBooks desktop, you must pay more fees to allow more people to use your book.

Comparing the price of QuickBooks online and QuickBooks desktop informs your decision on what to pick.

Installing QuickBooks Software

These accounting principles can be applied in QuickBooks for effective and efficient accounting processes. To download QuickBooks on a desktop, go to the download page on the QuickBooks website, to "Search" and "Download" your preferred version of QuickBooks Desktop. If the installation does not automatically start after download, select the QuickBooks product you downloaded on your desktop or the location you downloaded it. Select "Next" on the installation wizard.

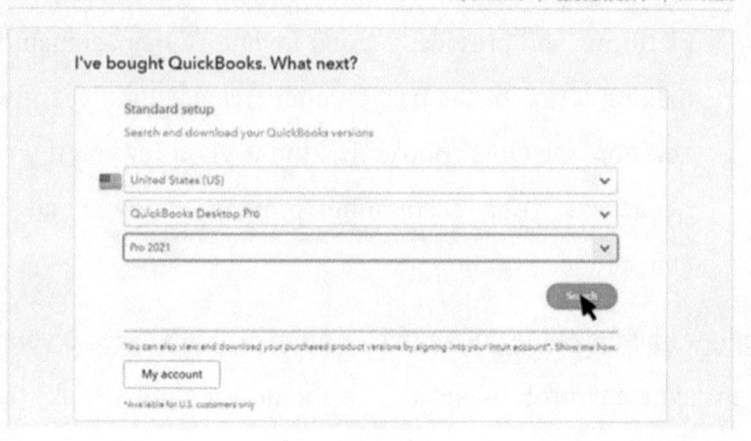

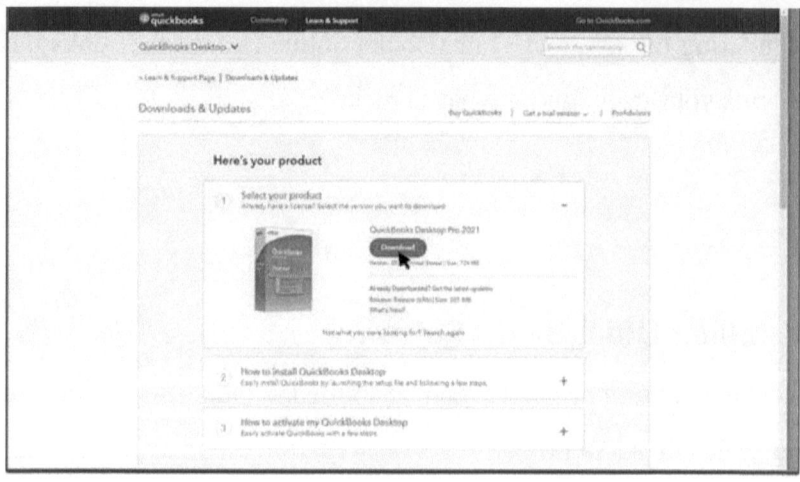

Here's your product

Agree to the software license agreement by selecting "Accept and Continue."

Input your license and product number after reading it. If unknown, select "Locate your license/product number" to access it.

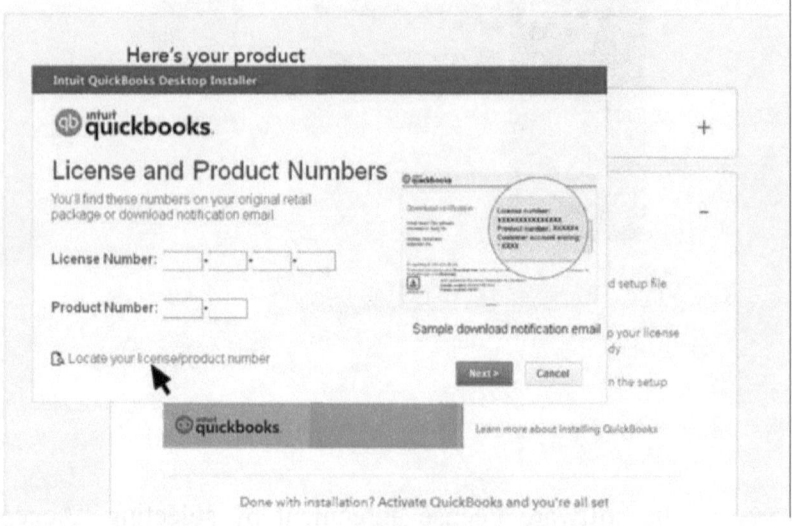

Choose your installation path. "Express" is recommended to be installed on the local stand-alone desktop. New users or individuals reinstalling QuickBooks should select this option too. If you want to change your QuickBooks location by connecting to a server or multi-user network, select "Custom and Network Options." Select "Next".

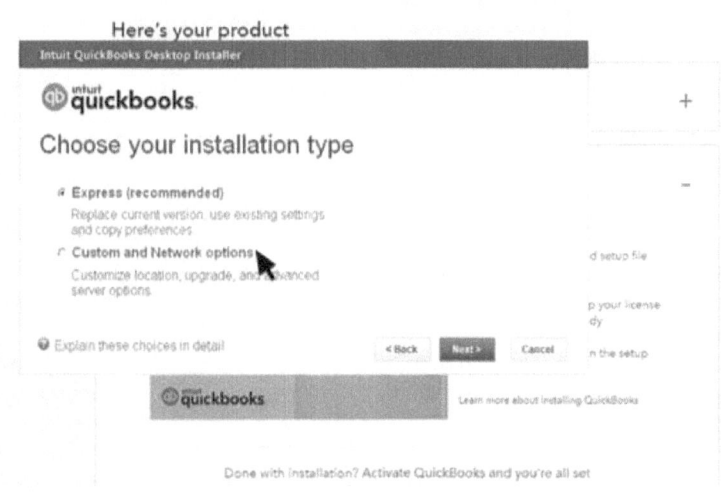

Select "Install" >" Open QuickBooks". If it is your first time installing QuickBooks on the computer, you will be prompted to reboot your computer to open the software. Activate QuickBooks for the maximal use of the software by clicking "Begin Activation." Once completed, you can use QuickBooks for your accounting processes.

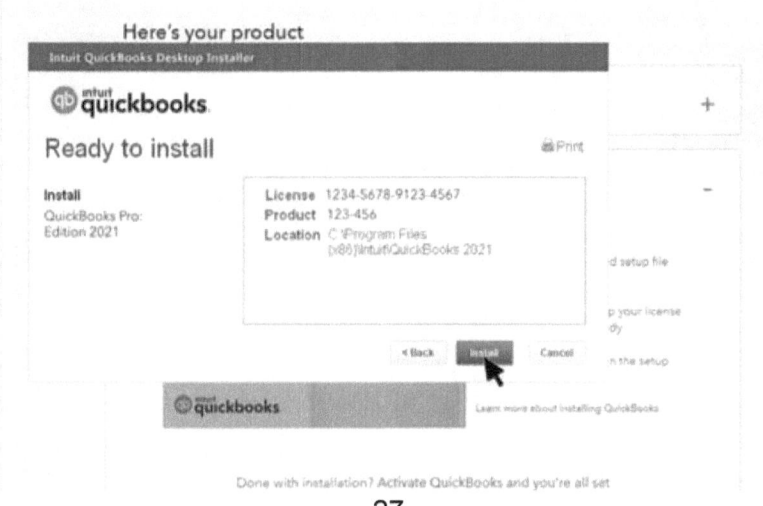

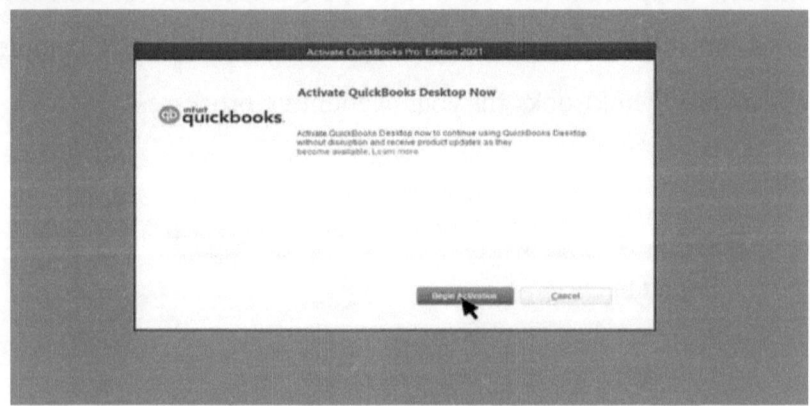

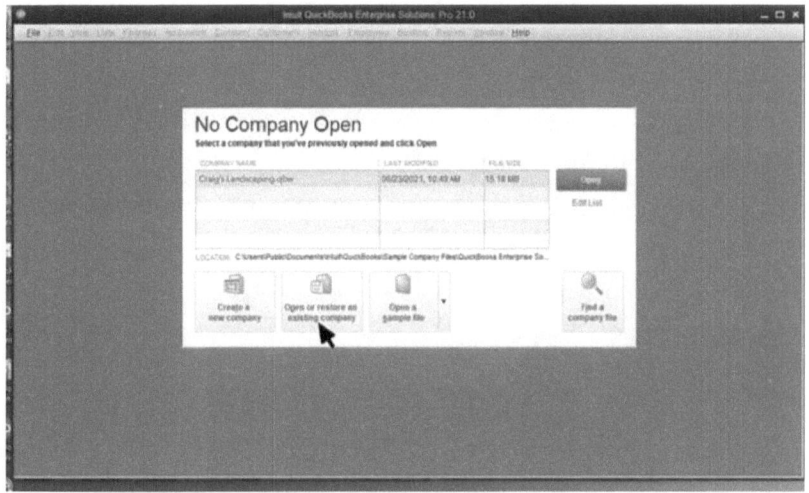

It should be noted that this illustration followed the "Express" installation path. If you select the Custom option, follow the instructions to connect you to a server and then install and activate. Installation of QuickBooks also requires an internet connection.

Setting up a new company file

After installation, start working with QuickBooks by creating a new file for your company. This file contains all the financial data and records of the company. For new beginners, open your freshly installed QuickBooks and select "Create a new company." However, you can create a new file for a new company anytime by going to the File menu and selecting the "New" option.

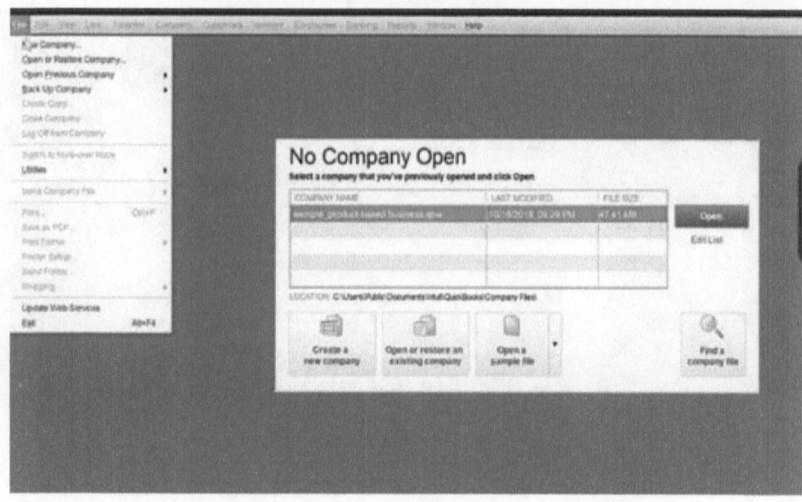

From there, select "Start Setup" in the dialog box opened.

Create an Intuit account with your email address if you do not already have one. If you do, skip this session.

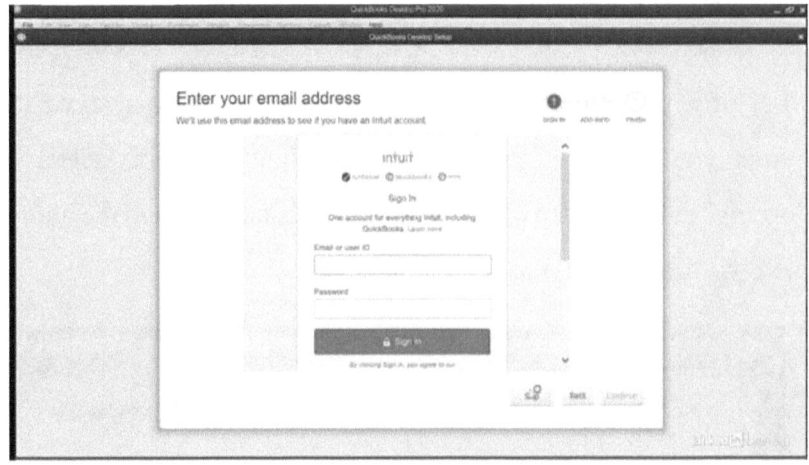

In the next section, you tell QuickBooks about the company by inputting your company's name, industry, and company type. These are the required questions. You can fill in other questions in this section later. Click "Create Company," and the company's file is created momentarily.

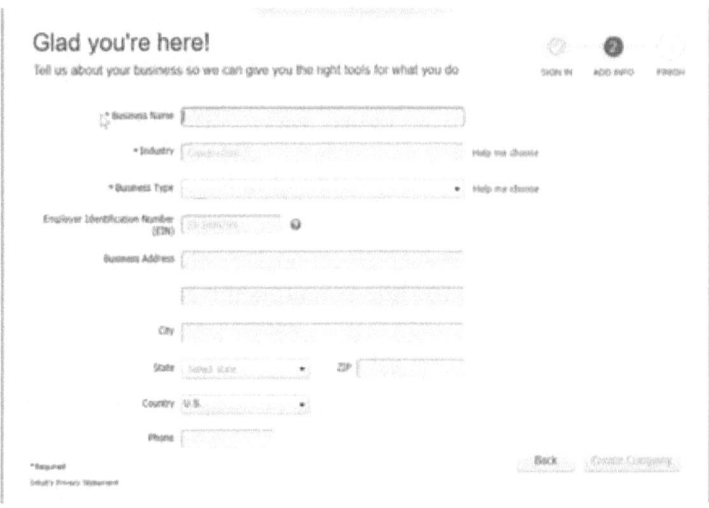

A list of additional services QuickBooks offers is displayed. Select anyone you are interested in. To get right to work, select "Start Working" at the bottom of this page, and this takes you to the homepage, where you can begin work immediately.

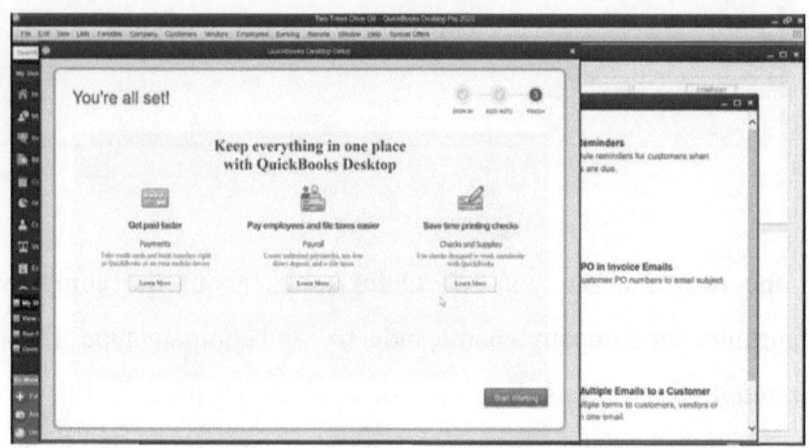

Navigating QuickBooks Interface

Getting familiar with QuickBooks and how it works to promote efficiency is important. The QuickBooks interface consists of different sections and icons. These icons represent the shortcuts to the accounting tools used in Excel. When QuickBooks Desktop is opened, the center of the large screen has two sections - the Home Page and Insights. To the left of the middle screen is the Icon bar. At the very top of the screen is the main Menu bar. The Menu bar possesses all the tools and features in the QuickBooks versions. They are arranged in categories. Hence, any feature not found in the icons of the Home Page and the Icon bar can be found in the Menu bar.

The Icon bar contains icons for any part of your company's financial file. It includes icons such as "My Shortcuts," where you add and access frequently used, and "View Balances," where you can view balances as the name implies. Also, the "Run favorite reports" and "Open Windows" icons with their name describing their functions. You can modify the content of these icons by selecting the "Customize..." button at the bottom of each icon when it is selected. The "Help/Search" icon is also present at the top of the Icon bar. Minimize and maximize the navigation pane or Icon bar by clicking on the "less than" symbol beside the "Help/Search" space. At the bottom of the Icon bar is a list of additional services of QuickBooks, which can be bought at any time. This section is in light blue. The cursor in the figure below points to this section.

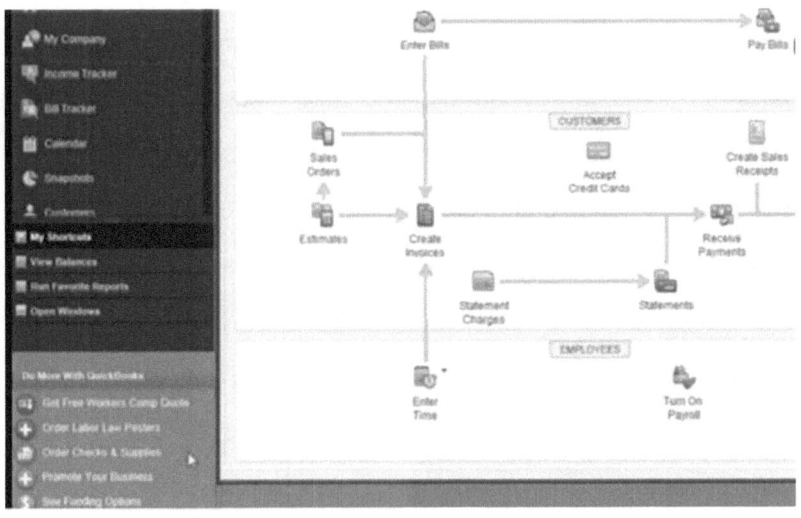

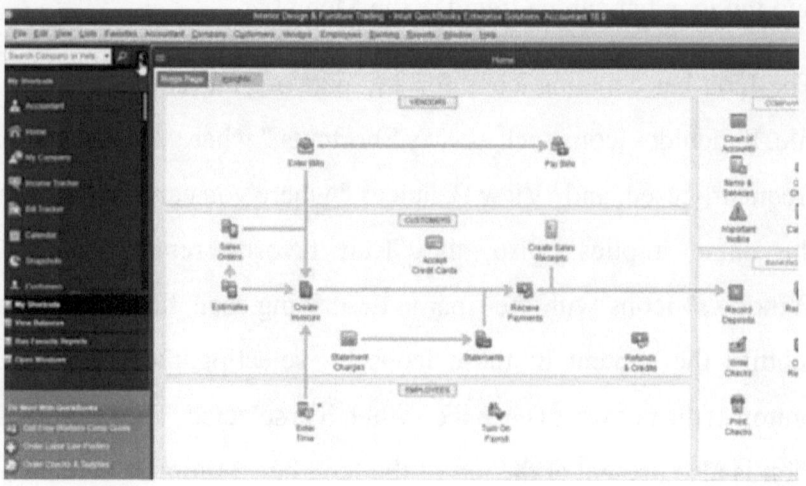

The Home Page is typically divided into three categories: "vendors," "customers," and "Employees." Each sector contains shortcut icons. Clicking on any category opens the company's information, where you can add or edit information relating to that category. For example, clicking "vendors" opens the recorded transactions and information relating to company vendors. The home page also displays icons connected with directional arrows under each category. The directional arrows tell how these shortcuts (icons) are interconnected within and across the different categories of inappropriate workflows. For example, once "Estimates" of a customer's transaction is made, the arrow shows that the next work is to "Create invoice." Also, in the case of a transaction with a vendor, once bills are entered, the next tool is to create an invoice (Entering Bills > Create invoice). To the right of the

Home Page are two more sections - Company and Banking. Icons in these sections also serve as shortcuts.

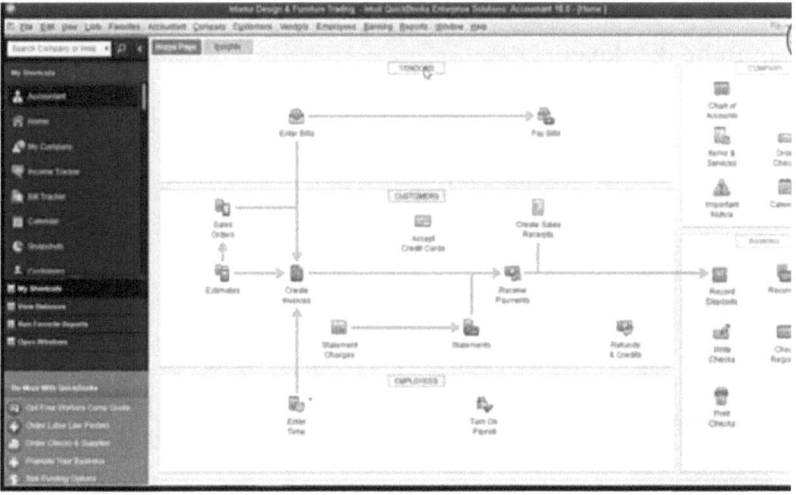

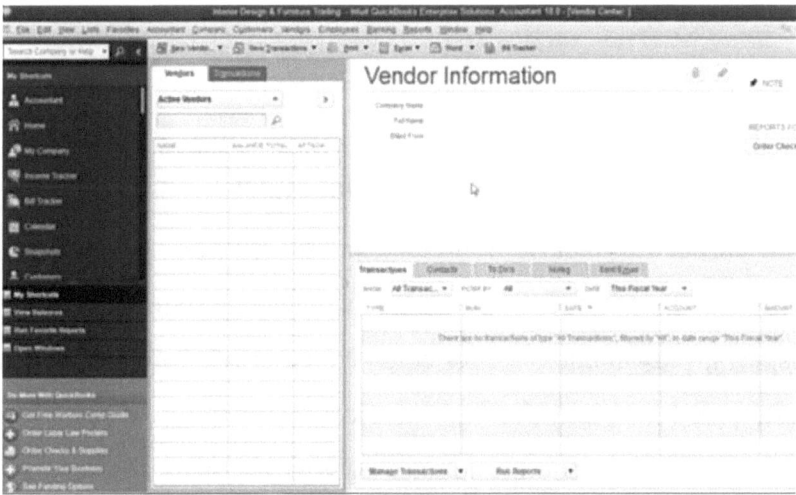

The Insights tab beside the Home Page shows visual representations (such as graphs) of financial insights gleaned from all the entries.

Showing how the company is fairing in business If it's gaining profits or losing. You can select the "Settings" symbol icon to customize your preferences and uncheck boxes representing the category you do not want to be displayed.

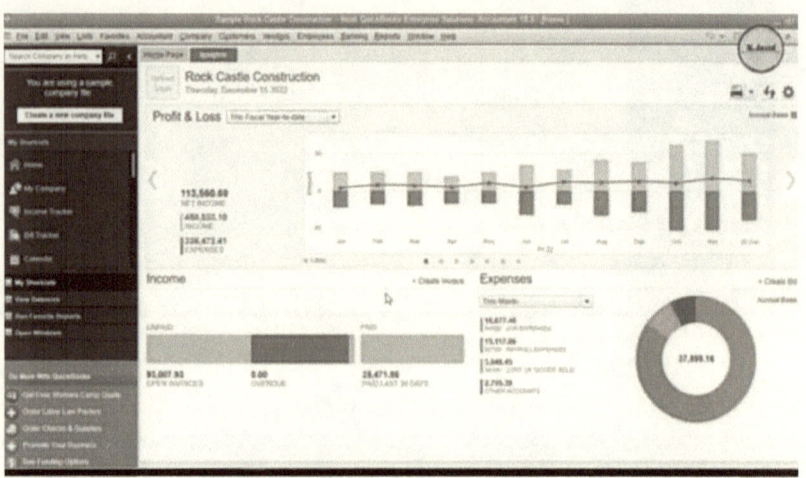

Customizing QuickBooks Preferences

You can set up QuickBooks to look and function how you want it to by using the "Preferences" feature. You can change some general desktop displays, play sounds, set up color icons, create backups, and create customized templates for your invoices, estimates, and sales receipts. You may also change the settings of your accounts and reports to fit your taste and the company's needs. All these and a lot more can be done with Preferences. Go to Edit > Preferences in the main Menu bar to customize your preferences. A long list of options you can adjust to your taste is on the left pane of the open Preferences window. They include Accounts, Reports, Desktop view, and General. The center of the Preferences windows had two tabs- "My Preferences" and "Company Preferences." Adjust QuickBooks to meet your wants, such as removing a warning, playing sound, or hiding the Home page in your desktop view. You can do this in the "My Preferences" section after selecting the related category you want to change (in the left pane). For example, to remove the Home page display from your desktop view, anytime you open QuickBooks, select Edit > Preferences > Desktop View > My Preferences, and then make the changes you want. However, if the change you want to make relates to the workflow of the company's file, make the changes in the "Company Preferences" tab. Click OK on the right pane to enact changes. Figures give a pictorial explanation of this.

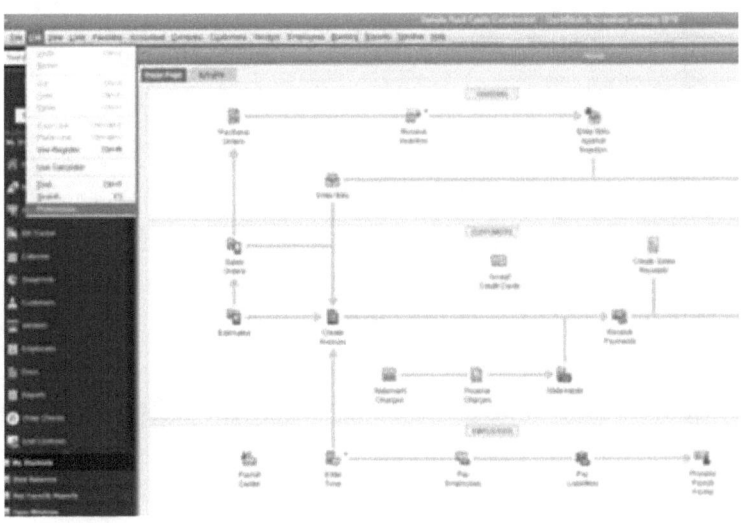

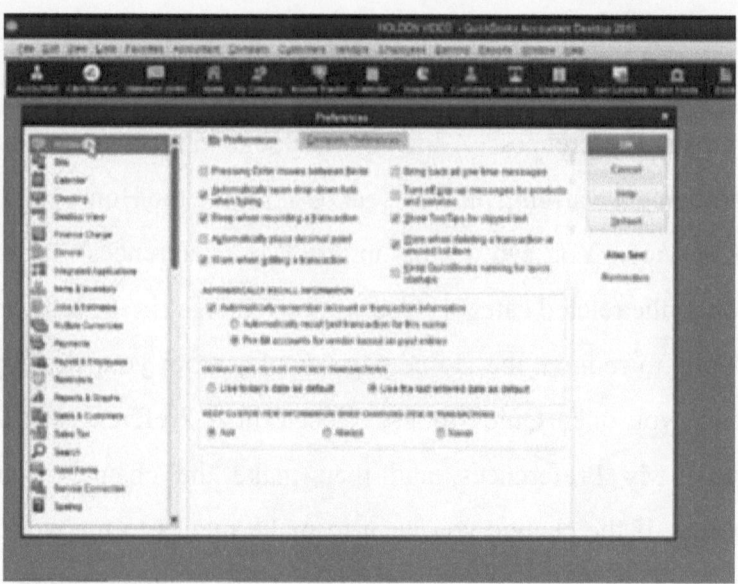

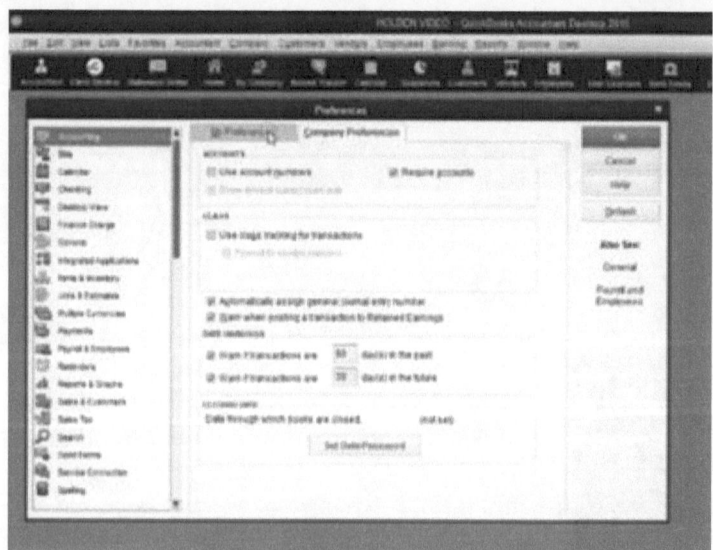

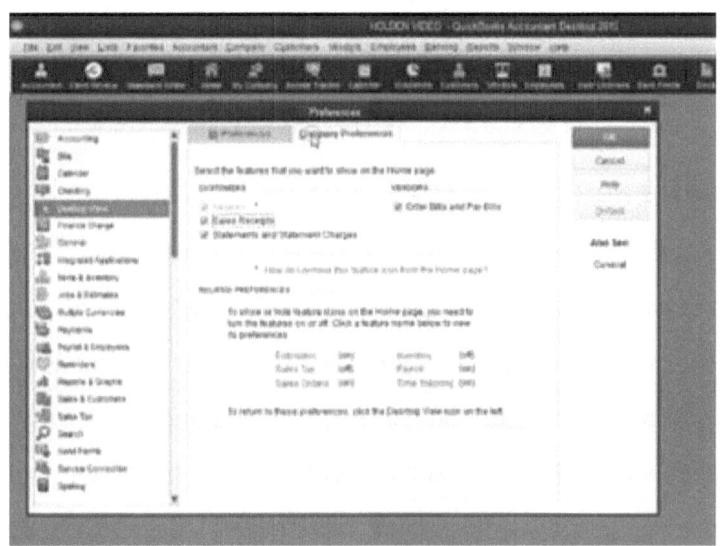

Chapter Three

Chart of Accounts and Lists

Creating and Managing Chart of Accounts

In QuickBooks, every account for your organization and its balance are listed in the chart of accounts. QuickBooks uses this list to keep track of cash, debts, and money coming in and going out and also organize your company's transactions on your reports and tax forms. Types of accounts in the chart of accounts include assets, liabilities, income, and expenses. QuickBooks has a particular set of standard accounts that it incorporates into a new chart of accounts created for a new company file. The type of account incorporated is based on what QuickBooks deems fit for the type of company or organization. However, you can also manually add another account that you need. The chart of accounts is divided into sections based on the type of account. Accounts in the chart of accounts can be edited, hidden, or deleted.

Adding an account

To manually add an account to your chart of accounts. From the main Menu, select **Lists > Chart of accounts**. Once the chart of accounts is opened, select the **Account** dropdown arrow at the bottom right corner of the chart of accounts. Select **New** in the accounting window that appears. Then, Input the new account details such as the name, type, and detailed type of account. Fill only options you are sure about, as the account details will influence QuickBook's interpretation of the

account, influencing the overall financial statement. Select **"Save &
close"** to complete an action.

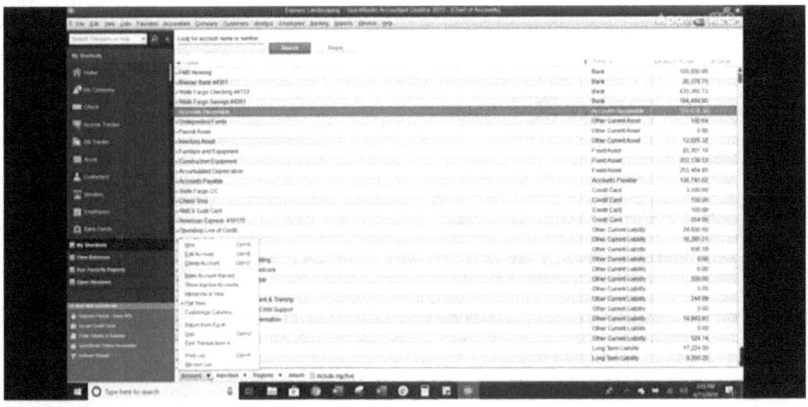

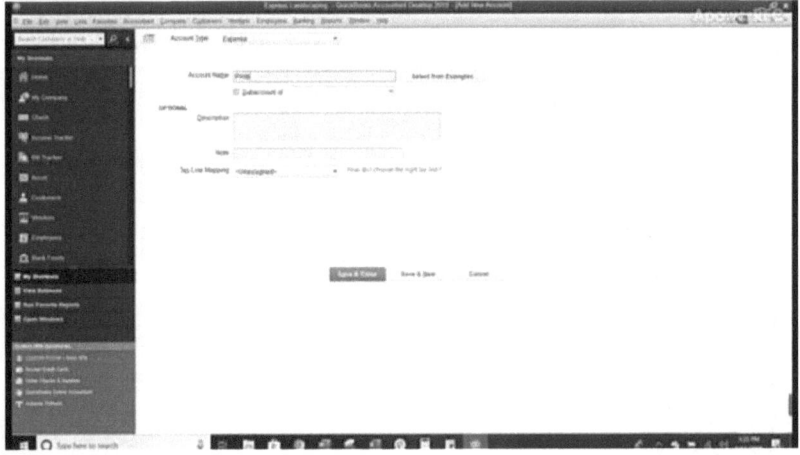

You may also add a subaccount. As the name suggests, a subaccount is
an account under another parent or main account. For instance, the gas
or telephone account is a subaccount of your utility account, which is
the main account. To add a subaccount, check the **Subaccount**
checkbox and select the parent account from the **Subaccount**
dropdown. Select **"Save & Close"**.

Edit an account

If you need to change the account details, open your chart of accounts from the **List** menu and right-click on the account you want to edit. Select **Edit Account** and make the changes you want to on account details. Select "**Save & Close**".

Delete an account

Only accounts without any activity history, like bank transactions, line items, or subaccounts, can be deleted from QuickBooks. To delete an account, go to **Lists > Chart of Accounts,** right-click on the account to be deleted, and select **Delete Account**. Select **OK**. If the account cannot be deleted, select the **"Make inactive"** option QuickBooks gives. Select this to inactivate the account.

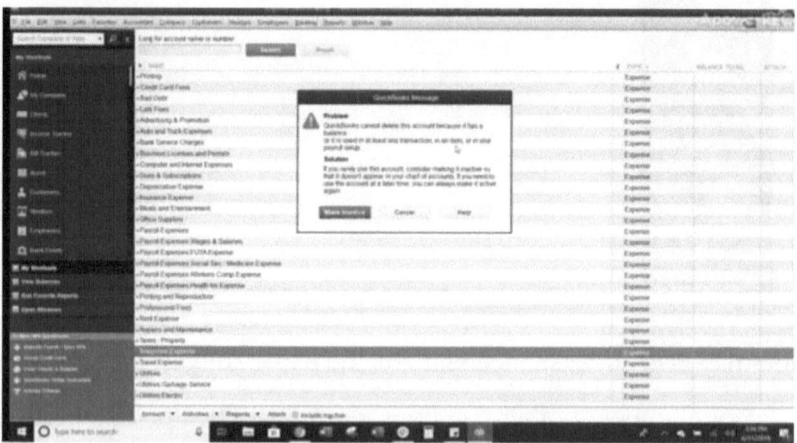

Inactivate an account.

When you inactivate an account, you hide it from your chart of accounts or financial sheet. You might want to inactivate an account to organize your chart intentionally. To do this, right-click on the account you want to inactivate and then select **Edit Account.** Check that the **Account is an inactive** checkbox, and then select "**Save & Close.**"

To reactivate the account, go to **Lists > Chart of Accounts.** Check the **Include inactive** checkbox, right-click on the account you want to reactivate, and click **Edit Account**. Uncheck the **Account is inactive** checkbox located at the bottom right corner of the chart of accounts. Select "**Save & Close**". You can also just go ahead and uncheck the box in front of the account you want to reactivate right after selecting the **Include inactive**.

Add account numbers

In QuickBooks, you can add account numbers to identify the type of account easily. For instance, this lets you know if the account is an asset, a liability, or an expense or income account. To do this, go to **Preferences** in the **Edit** menu, select **Accounting** in the left pane, and select the **Company Preferences** tab. Check the "**Use account number**" tab checkbox and select **OK**.

Working with Customers and Jobs

You can perform every activity related to your customers through the **Customer Centre.** Once you create a new company file, you can fill in the information about your customers and jobs on the customer's or customer's job lists. You can also include customers with pending payments, so you have a proper account of customer's information. To add a new customer to your Customers and Jobs list, click the Customers button in the Icon or Menu bar. Then click the **Customer Centre**. You can also use the Customers shortcut on the Home page or the **Ctrl + J** shortcut to go to the Customer Centre. Click the New **Customer & Job** dropdown in the menu at the top of the Customers Centre window and select the **New Customer** choice. You can then enter data on the new customer you want to add. Amongst many others, these data include the name, contact, shipping address, billing preferences, and specific sales tax of the customer. You can also create customized information you want displayed for all your customers.

The **Customers & Jobs** tab is located on the left side of the Customer Centre windows. It is one of the most basic and important aspects of the Customer Centre window as it bears the list of all your customer's information and the jobs done for them. When you click on any customer or job in the **Customers & Jobs,** its information and transactions are displayed at the center of the Customer Centre window. Just like in the chart of accounts, you can edit information of customers inactivate or delete a customer's information from the customers (or jobs) list in this tab. The steps to do these are also similar to those in the chart of accounts. For example, to edit information about a particular customer, right-click the customer's name in the **Customers & Jobs** list and click **Edit** in the menu that pops up, or double-click on the customer or job name, and you can also select the **pencil** icon (the edit symbol) besides its information displayed in the Customer Centre window. All these take you to the **Edit Customer** window, where you can make the changes you want and click **OK** to save changes. This way, you can add a new job to the customer's information or edit an existing job. Inactivate by checking the **Include inactive** checkbox in the Edit Customer window. Right-click on the customer name, select **Delete** to delete a customer and press **OK** to confirm delete. Also, note that only customers without any transactions can be deleted.

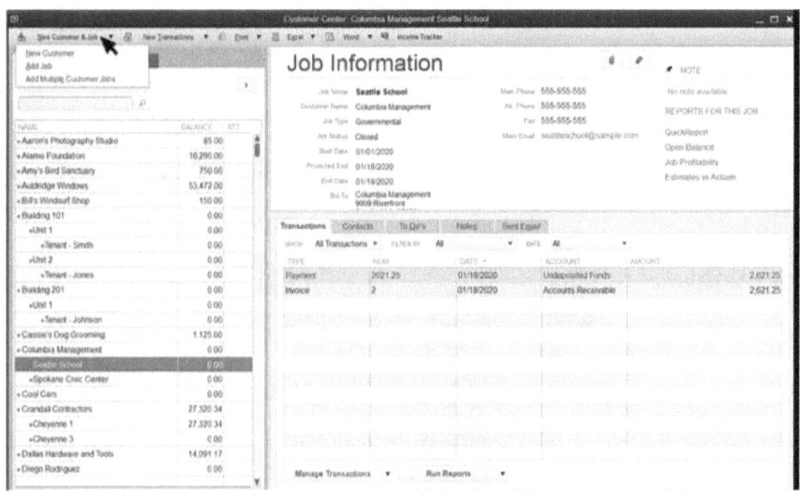

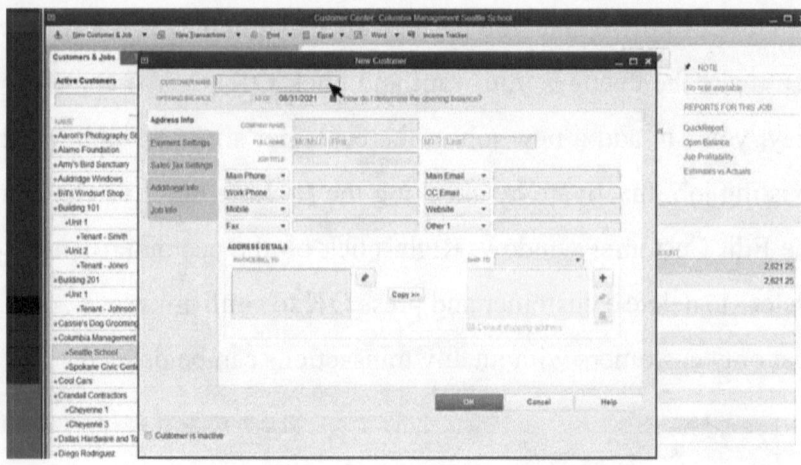

Finally, you can manage your customer list on QuickBooks by tracking customers' invoices and payments over a specific period. To do this, go to the **Reports** tab on the main Menu bar, select **Customers and Receivables**, and then select Transaction list by customers in the next menu. Adjust the date to the period you want to track, and a list of all customer transactions made within the period is seen. This way, you can check and correct all customer-related transactions in reports.

Managing Vendors and Suppliers

After creating a new company file on QuickBooks, it is important to record the purchases made and the vendors they are purchased from. This will make up your QuickBooks Vendors list. This list helps you to track your purchases and helps you know who you are to pay and what you are paying them for. This management list also helps you to know the vendors you are issuing a 1099-MISC at the end of the calendar year. To add a vendor to your company's file Vendors list, select **Vendors** on the Icon or Menu bar, then select **Vendors Centre**. Select the **New Vendor** dropdown in the vendor center menu list to set up a new vendor. Enter every information of vendor required. These include the name, contact information, eligibility for form 1099-MISC, and payment preferences. Click **OK** to confirm the vendor set up process. This new vendor now appears on the Vendors list of company file. Subsequently, you can modify a vendor's information by navigating to the **Edit Vendor** widow. However, you can edit, inactivate, and delete a vendor by navigating the same steps in managing Customers and Jobs in correspondence with vendors. For instance, to locate the Vendors lists in the Vendors Center window, select the **Vendors** icon on the main menu or icon bar instead of the Customers icon.

To track an incorrect balance detail associated with Vendors transactions, select **Vendor Center** in the **Vendors** menu. Select any suspected vendor with the wrong transaction from the Vendors list and go to the **Transactions** tab on the right. Click the **Show** dropdown, then the **Balance Details**. This will show the balance for that transaction, and you can crosscheck errors. You can also narrow down the suspected transactions by time of time, using the **Filter by** and **Date** dropdown arrows to select the time range. If the balance is higher than expected, you may have made payments via a route not recognized by QuickBooks (e.g., using checks instead of the Pay Bills window. If the balance is unexpectedly low, even without obvious outstanding payment, you may have entered the wrong amount at the transaction entry. You can also track the vendor's payments for a selected time frame by navigating the **Reports** menu to **Vendors and Payables** and then **Vendors balance detail**. Set the time frame you want to track at the top of this page, and the appropriate list will appear. You can also track other groups of vendors in the Reports menu. For instance, select "**Reports > Vendors and Payables >1099** Summary" to track vendors with 1099 issuance.

Generally, and also in QuickBooks, vendors and suppliers have identical meanings. However, vendors are used in QuickBooks Desktop (Windows and Mac), while suppliers are used to represent vendors in QuickBooks Online. To locate the Suppliers list on QuickBooks Online, select **Expenses**, and then click **Suppliers** from the menu that appears. You can set up, add, and edit your suppliers list by intuitively navigating icons.

Setting up products and Services

Products and services in QuickBooks fall under the **Items and Services** element of the company's file. These Items and services include anything (tangible products and services) a company purchases, sells and resells. They include items and services bought from vendors and those offered, sold, or resold to customers. Once you have your vendors and customers list, creating the list of items and services you deal with before entering any transaction is important. This way, QuickBooks can set up and interpret your transactions' elements. Items and Services include goods or products, shipping fees, discounts, and sales taxes (when applicable). Just like account types, items, and services are classified under different types or categories such as Service (services provided to a customer), Inventory part (products bought to sell), Non-inventory part (products purchased but not resold or those sold but not purchased), and Other charges. Subtotals, Discounts, Payments, and so on.

To set up or add an item, go to **Lists** and then select the **Item List** tab, or go to the **Items and Services** shortcut on the Home page. Then select the **Item** dropdown arrow at the bottom right corner of the Item List, then select **New**. Input information on new items such as the name, description, and type of item. Go to the Custom Fields to add your own customized fields. Then select **Save**. To keep adding items, select **Next** instead of Save. This opens the New Item window for you to create another item.

You can also add an item on the invoice or any other sales form by simply adding the name of a new item and selecting **Yes** when asked if you want to set up the new item. Edit an item's information on the Item List by double-clicking on the item you want to change, making changes in the Edit Item window, and selecting **OK**. To merge a duplicate entry in the Item list, go to the Item list and copy the name of the item you want to keep. Then right-click on the name of the item you do not want to keep, select **Edit**, paste the name you copied in the Item name tab, select **Save & Close**, and select Yes when asked if you want to merge the list. You can also merge duplicate entries in your chart of accounts, vendor lists, and customer lists in this manner. Also, in the same manner, you can hide (inactive) and delete an item like in the other lists.

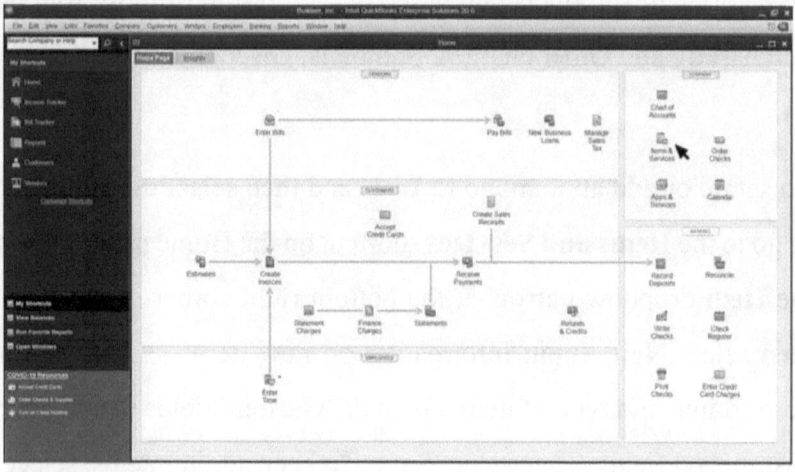

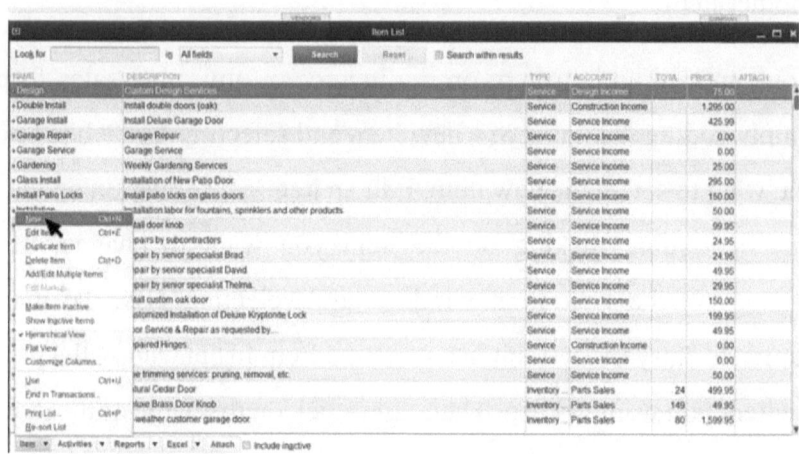

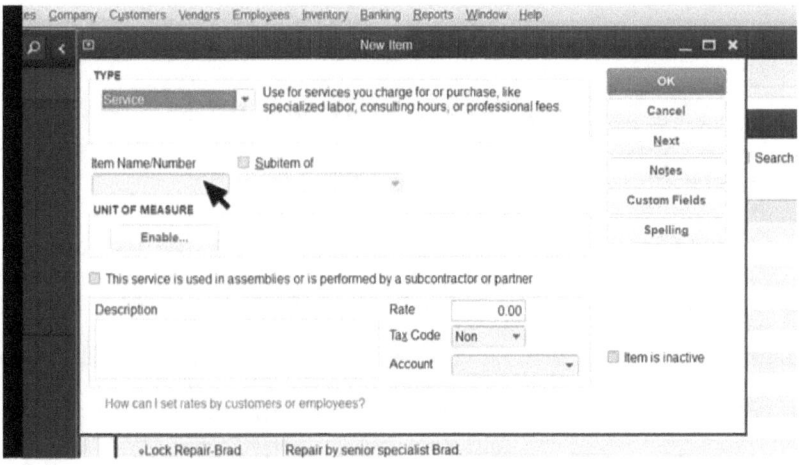

New Item

TYPE

Service

Use for services you charge for or purchase, like specialized labor, consulting hours, or professional fees.

OK

Cancel

Next

Notes

Custom Fields

Spelling

Search

Item Name/Number ☐ Subitem of

UNIT OF MEASURE

Enable...

☐ This service is used in assemblies or is performed by a subcontractor or partner

Description

Rate 0.00

Tax Code Non ▼

Account

☐ Item is inactive

How can I set rates by customers or employees?

◦Lock Repair-Brad | Repair by senior specialist Brad.

51

Chapter Four

Entering Transactions

Recording sales and invoices

The **Sales Order, Sales Receipt,** and **Creating invoices** are all sales records in QuickBooks. The Sales Order is a form showing a customer's order or orders which can be saved and sent to the customer to verify the order before the order is delivered. The Sales receipt records customers' sales that pay immediately after services or product is delivered, such as a restaurant. This form can also emailed or printed out for the customer. An invoice is a form that contains the details of the customer's orders and payment preferences and the date created and sent after the order has been delivered. The windows of these three sales forms are similar in QuickBooks. They comprise the Customer's information, an item table, and a footer containing other miscellaneous information. You can customize the layout of your sales, sales receipt, and invoice to your taste, selecting the features you want to show or hide in the form sent to the customer.

To create a Sales Order, select the **Sales Order** tab in the **Customer** menu and enter the customer and item you want to create. QuickBooks fills in the other details of the customer and the item selected. However, the inputs can be manually done and also edited.

Select **Formatting > Customize Page layout** to make personal changes to your sales order. Click **Save & Close** to save the entry. You can create an invoice for a Sales Order created and fulfilled by selecting **Create Invoice** from the **Main** tab.

If you have not created or fulfilled a Sales Order, create an invoice by selecting **Create Invoices** from the Home page shortcut or **Create Invoices** in the **Customer** main menu. Enter the customer and item for which you want to create an invoice. Customize the page layout if you want to. Select **Save & Close**.

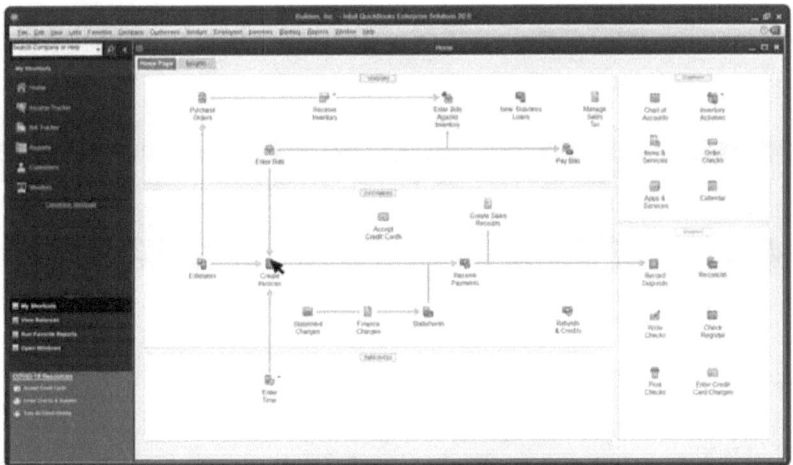

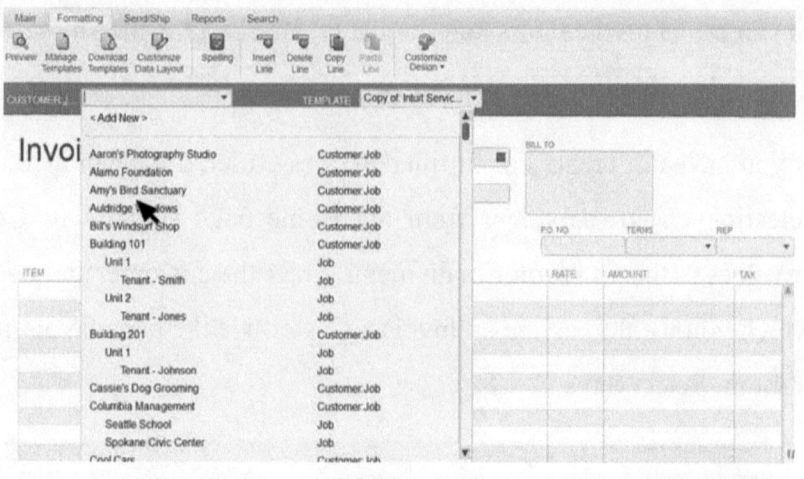

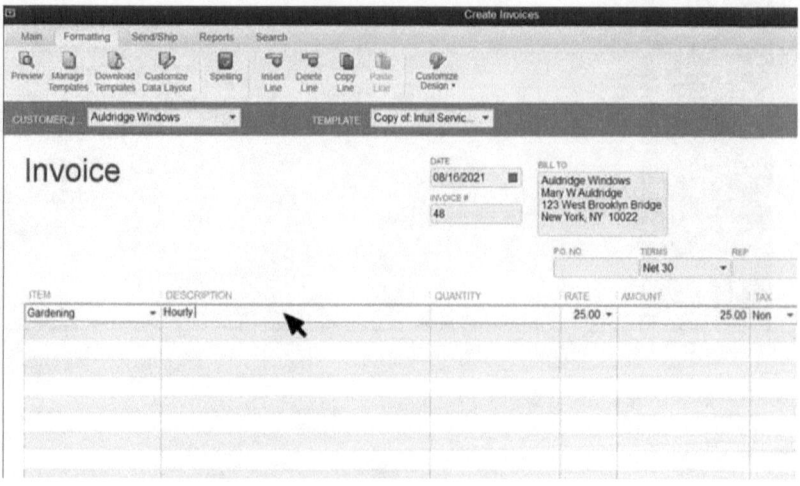

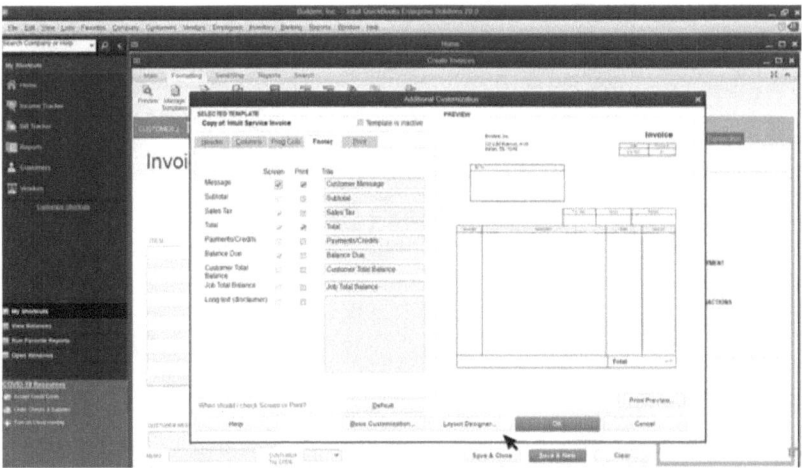

Once you have received payment for sales, you can create, send, or print sales receipts by selecting **Create Sales Receipt** on the Home page. Fill in the information for the transaction in the Sales Receipt window that opens.

Managing Expenses and Purchase Orders

It is also essential to enter and save company expenses and purchase transactions in QuickBooks. General expenses are recorded by entering their means of payment. To record a check payment, select **Check Register** in the "**Banking**" section of the Home page or the main menu. Select the bank account charged from the dialogue box at the top of the **Check Register** windows and a new blank row is opened to enter other transaction information (such as the date and amount of payment, vendor, payee, check reference number, appropriate account form chart of accounts) of the new transaction. Click **Record** to save the transaction. You can also select the Write Checks icon to record your check transactions.

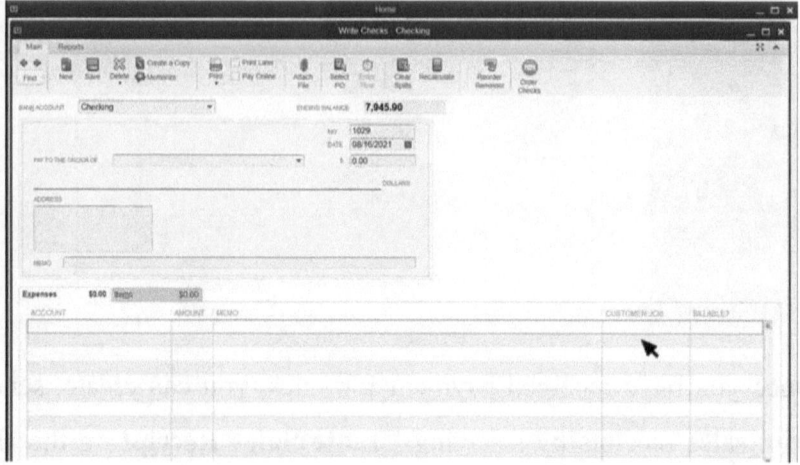

To record an expense charged to a credit card, select **Credit card charges** in the Banking section or menu. Enter the credit card used at the top of the screen and other necessary information relating to the transaction. Click **Save & Close** to save the transaction. Select Save and New to save the transaction and enter a new transaction immediately.

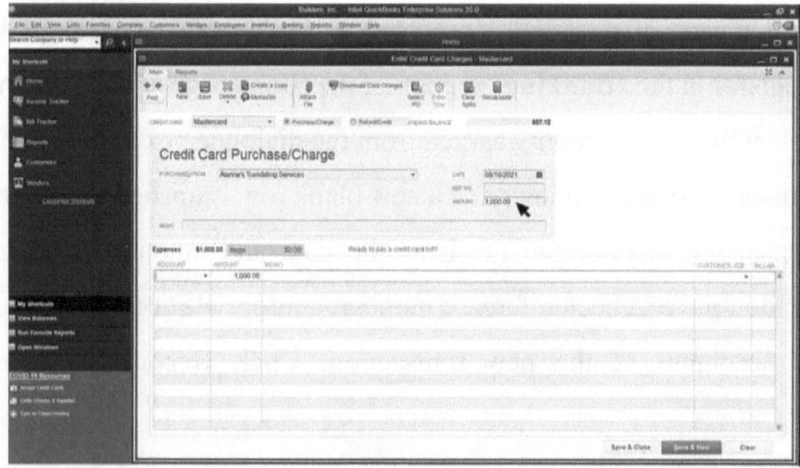

You can also create a list of purchase orders to keep track of purchases. To turn on purchase orders, check the **Inventory and purchase orders are active** checkbox in the **Company Preferences** tab of the **Items & Inventory** option in the **Preferences** window. Once purchase orders are activated, click **Vendors** > **Create Purchase Orders** to begin creating Purchase Orders. Continue by clicking the **Vendor** dropdown to select the vendor you want to create a purchase order. Select **Add New** to add a new vendor. Enter the other relevant information (such as the item purchased). Select **Save & Close**. You can also create a purchase order from created estimates by selecting **Create Purchase Order** in the **Estimates** window. View and track all Purchase Orders from the **Lists** or **Reports** menu. Use the Enter Bill > Pay Bills workflow to record vendor credit purchases. When the vendor sends you an invoice, you enter bills, and after payment, you enter the transaction in Pay Bills.

Handling Banks and Credit Card Transactions

Two major ways to record your company's bank transactions are in its QuickBooks file. One, you can connect the company's bank accounts or credit cards to QuickBooks so that QuickBooks automatically sees and records every transaction. To do this, go to "**Banking**" on the menu, select **Bank Feeds**, and then select **"Set up a bank feed for an account."** Enter your bank's or credit card company's name in the Bank Feed Setup widow. You can select from the list of common financial institutions QuickBooks provides. On the next field, enter the username and password of your online banking account and other security details required. After this, your different bank accounts or credit cards in the company are displayed.

You can then select which of them to link to your QuickBooks account. To add a bank account without a corresponding account in the chart of accounts, select the account and select **Create New Account** in the list that appears. Create the new account, and then select **Connect** to link bank account (s). Once the connection is complete, all transactions of the bank account or credit card connected appear on QuickBooks. Categorize them so QuickBooks adds them to your accounts. The second way is to manually upload a file containing the bank account's or credit card's financial statements to QuickBooks. This way, QuickBooks can generate reports with it.

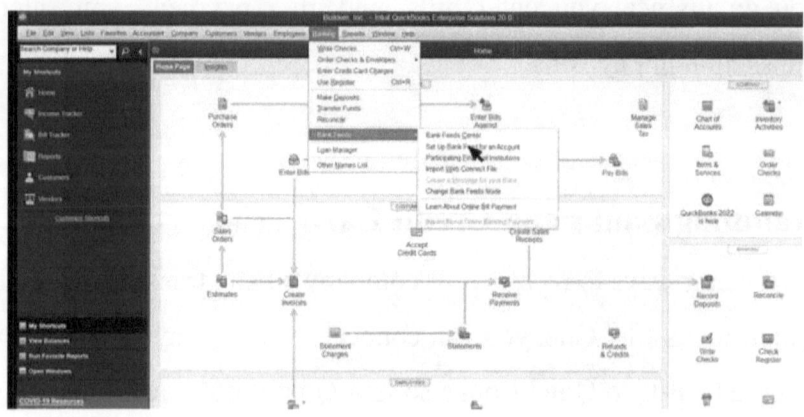

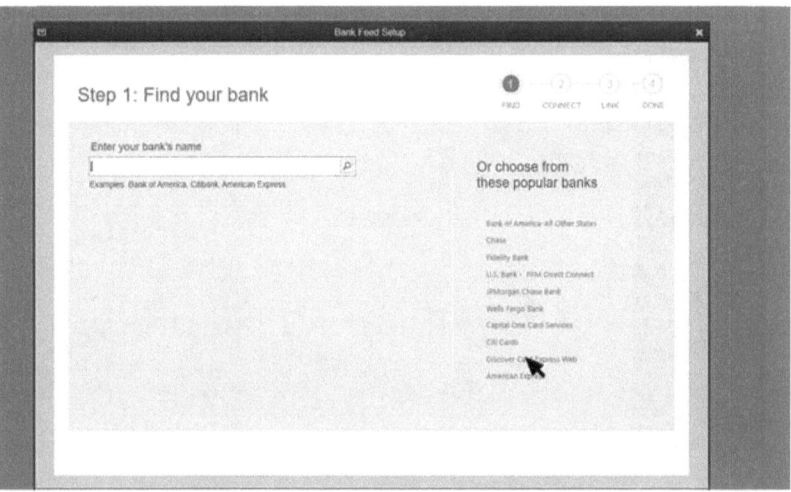

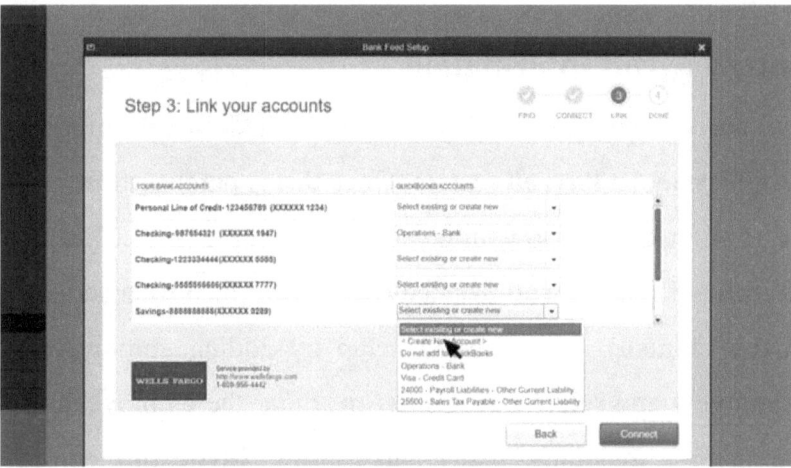

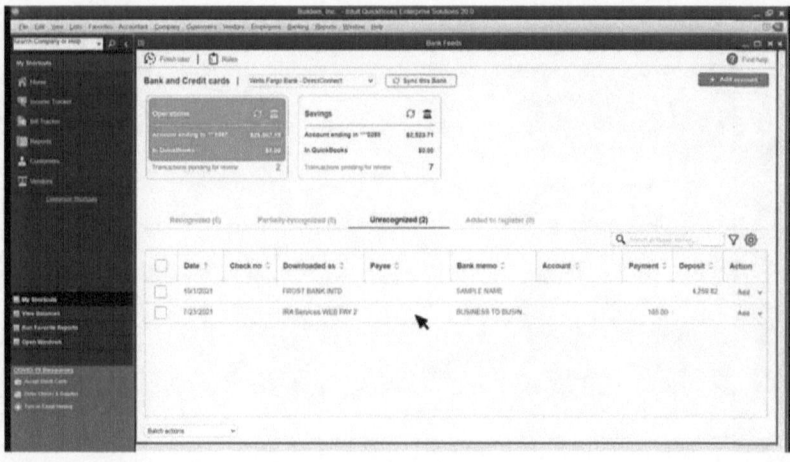

Enter Payroll Information

You need a QuickBooks Desktop Payroll add-on subscription to use the QuickBooks **Payroll** feature. Once this is purchased, activate with the 16-digit key sent to your email after purchase (select **Employees** > **Payroll** > **Enter Payroll Service Key** > **Add** (then enter service key) > **Next** > **Finish**). Start Payroll setup by adding employees. Go to **Employees** and select **Payroll Setup**. Enter the employee's principal information, including their email address. **Invite this employee to enter the personal details** box if you want them to. Select Next to fill in the Pay Details field, and select **Next** to fill in the **Personal Details** field. Do this till all fields on employees' details are filled. Then select **"Done"**. Select **Run Payroll** if you have not paid any employees for the year. On the left pane of the **QuickBooks Payroll Setup** window, select the **Company** icon to set up your company compensation items for employees, such as retirement deductions and insurance benefits. You can also enter the list of employees paid before the payroll is set up by selecting the **Pay History** icon. Set up employee's taxes, review and finalize set up by selecting the corresponding icon.

If you have not subscribed to the enhanced Payroll service of QuickBooks, you can manually input employee information by selecting **Edit** > **Preferences** > **Payroll & Employees** > **Company Preferences**. Check the Full Payroll and Manual Payroll checkboxes in the Payroll Features section. Select **Next** and then **Activate**. Click **OK** to enact changes.

Reconciling and Reporting

Reconciling Bank and Credit Card Accounts
It is important to reconcile QuickBooks banking reports with real-life bank statements. This is best done monthly. To reconcile an account in QuickBooks, access your bank account or credit card statements from

the bank website and upload them on QuickBooks. Then select **Banking** > **Reconcile** or **Reconcile** shortcut on the home page. Enter the name of the bank or credit card account you want to reconcile, the **Ending Date** and **Beginning Date** (of the uploaded financial statement you want to reconcile with), and other necessary information, such as bank charges. The left table shows activities such as checks and payments that decreased your bank balance, while the right shows deposits and other credits that increase your balance. Select any transaction reconciling with the financial statement and click the Match icon. Enter the **Ending date** of the reconciliation, and all the matching transactions to that date are checked. Unchecked transactions can be reviewed to correct errors in amount entry and other errors. Double-click any wrong entry, and make the correct entry. Compare until the difference in balance shows zero. Then click **Reconcile Now** to complete reconciliation.

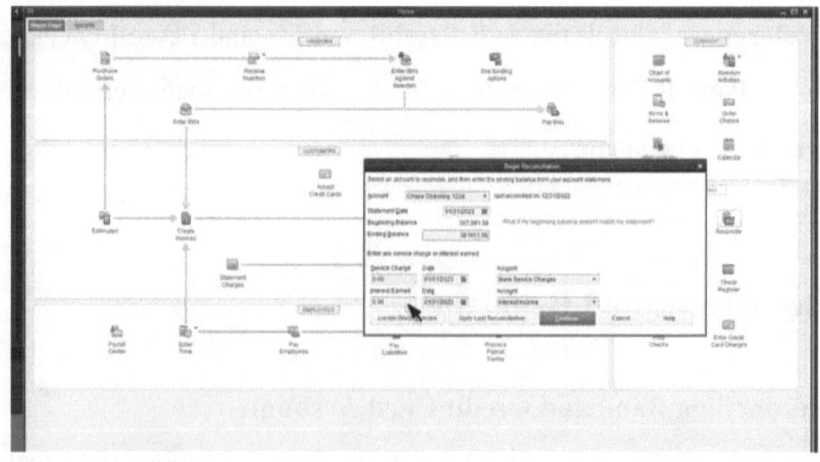

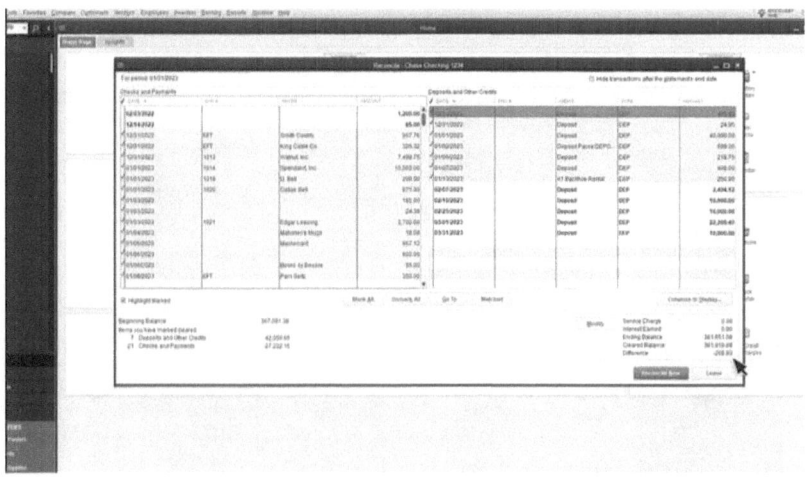

Generating Financial Statements

QuickBooks can generate three primary financial statements: Profit and Loss Statement, Balance Sheet, and Cash flow statements.

To generate your Profit and Loss statement, called the Income statement, go to **Reports** > **Company and Financial** > **Profit & Loss Standard**. The profit and loss report opens. You can edit and customize the report template to meet your needs by clicking on the Customize Report menu. This report can be emailed, printed, and even exported to Excel Spreadsheet for more analysis.

Navigate through the **Reports** menu similarly and click on **Balance Sheet Standard** to view the Company's balance sheet and the **Cash Flow Standard** to view a report on the company's cash flow. You can also track, send, print, and customize the Balance Sheet and Cash Flow statement templates.

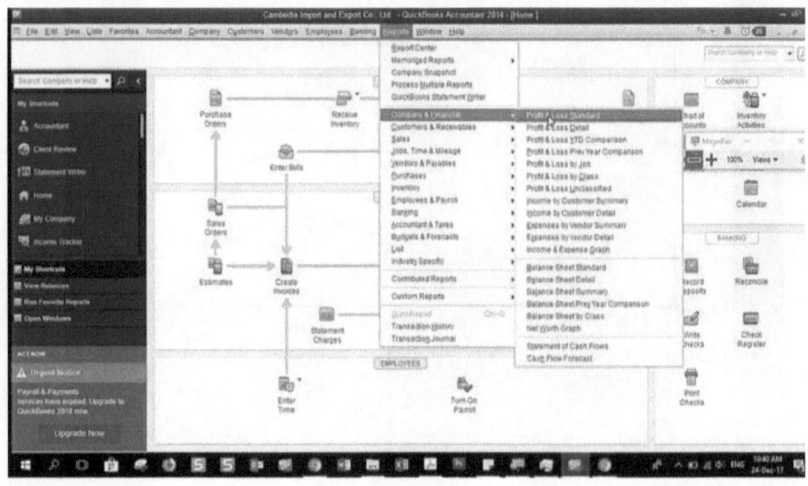

Customizing Reports for Business Analysis

QuickBooks Desktop enables you to customize any report generated for specific or general financial and business analysis. You can customize the report by choosing a specific time range or the elements you want displayed in the column of the report sheet. The balance sheet and profit and loss statements are two common financial reports analyzed. The former tells you how much assets, liabilities, and equity a company possesses, while the latter shows a company's income and expenses rate. Click the **Customize Report** to make changes to the arrangement and elements of a report. For example, to view a business' Profit and Loss report throughout the months of a year, select the Customize Report menu, set the Date tab to **"This Fiscal year-to-Date,"** and enter the specific dates in the **From** and **To** tabs. You can set Column Display by Months in the Columns section and select **OK**.

Only the transaction details for these months are displayed as customized, allowing you to track income and carry out major analyses. The figure below illustrates this example.

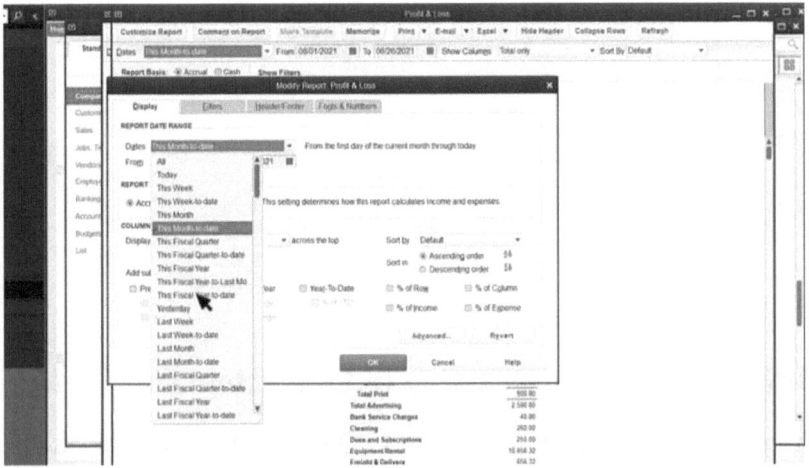

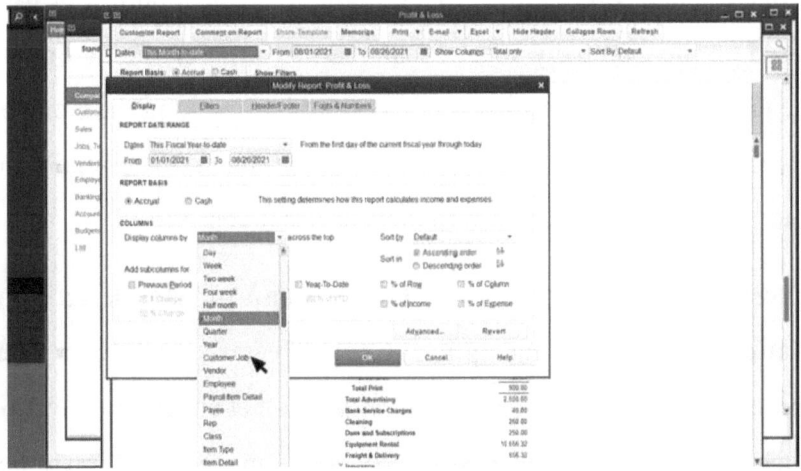

Budgeting and Forecasting in QuickBooks

From a company's financial data, QuickBooks can also help with budgeting and forecasting. For example, to create a budget or forecast based on the Company's last fiscal year, ensure that the first month of the last fiscal year is set up (Budgetrectly by checking the Company > My Company > Edit > Report Information menu). The report should also be correctly customized to the last fiscal year.

To create a budget, go to the **Company menu** and then select from the **Planning & Budgeting** option. Click Create New Budget. Set the appropriate fiscal year for the budget and select either Profit & Loss or Balance Sheet, then select Next. Select if you want to "Create budget from scratch" or "Create budget from the previous year's actual data." Click Finish to complete. Navigate through QuickBooks the same to create a forecast (Company > Planning & Budgeting > Setup Forecast > Create New Forecast). You can review your budgets or forecasts in the Budgets and Forecasts of the Reports menu.

Chapter Five

Payroll and Taxes

Setting Up Payroll in QuickBooks

Payroll is essential to any business; efficient management is crucial for smooth operations. QuickBooks, a popular accounting software, offers a comprehensive payroll feature that simplifies the process. Setting up payroll in QuickBooks involves several steps that ensure accurate and timely employee payment.

The first step in setting up payroll is to gather all necessary information about your employees, such as their names, addresses, social security numbers, tax withholding information, and pay rates. This data will be used to create employee profiles within QuickBooks.

Next, you need to set up your company's payroll preferences. This includes choosing the appropriate payroll schedule (weekly, bi-weekly, monthly), determining how often you want payroll to run (e.g., every Friday), and choosing how to pay your employees (direct deposit or check printing).

After setting these options, you can import employee information into QuickBooks by adding them one at a time or importing data from an external source such as an Excel spreadsheet. You can begin processing payroll once all employee records are created and checked for accuracy.

QuickBooks allows you to manually enter each employee's hours or import them from a time-tracking system. The software then calculates the total salary based on the salary entered during setup. After total wages are calculated, deductions such as taxes and benefits can be applied automatically using the tax tables provided by QuickBooks or custom settings based on your specific needs.

Finally, after verifying the accuracy of all calculations and making any necessary adjustments or corrections, you can create paychecks directly for your employees through QuickBooks. The software also generates detailed summary reports of each paycheck issued. In short, setting up payroll in QuickBooks helps streamline the process of paying employees accurately and efficiently. By diligently following these steps and ensuring accurate data entry throughout the setup process, businesses can save time and resources while remaining compliant with legal requirements related to money management wages.

Processing Employee Payroll and Taxes

Companies must effectively manage employee payroll and taxes in today's fast-paced business world. Quickbooks, a popular accounting software, offers a comprehensive solution to streamline these processes.

First, QuickBooks simplifies payroll by automatically calculating and generating paychecks. It allows businesses to easily create employee profiles with relevant information such as salary, deductions, and tax deductions. With just a few clicks, employers can generate accurate employee paychecks, saving valuable time and reducing the risk of errors.

Quickbooks integrates with tax agencies' systems to ensure accurate tax calculations and timely payments. It automatically calculates federal and state taxes based on the latest regulations, eliminating the need for manual calculations or hiring external tax professionals. This saves costs and minimizes the chances of penalties or audits due to incorrect filings.

Quickbooks provides detailed reports that help businesses track payroll expenses effectively.

Employers can access reports on wages paid, taxes withheld, and other related data anytime. These reports enable better financial planning by providing information about labor costs and helping businesses make informed decisions about budgets or staffing.

Processing payroll and employee taxes in Quickbooks brings many benefits to businesses. From simplifying payroll to ensuring accurate tax reporting and providing in-depth reporting, this software improves efficiency while reducing costs and risks associated with manual or support processes. Therefore, adopting Quickbooks is highly recommended for businesses looking for an effective solution to manage salaries and taxes for their employees.

Managing Payroll Liabilities

Payroll is essential to any business, and managing payroll costs is vital to maintaining financial stability. QuickBooks, a widely used accounting software, offers several tools and features to streamline this process. One of the key features of QuickBooks is the ability to calculate payroll taxes accurately. The software automatically calculates federal and state taxes, Social Security, Medicare, and other deductions based on employee information. This eliminates the need for manual calculations and reduces the risk of errors.

QuickBooks also allows users to create liability accounts to track payroll obligations separately. This allows businesses to monitor their tax obligations and ensure timely payments effectively. Users can easily generate reports that provide a comprehensive overview of all payroll obligations, making financial data analysis easier.

Another benefit of using QuickBooks to manage payroll obligations is integration with electronic payment systems. The software allows users to deposit money directly or pay debts electronically through the system itself. This not only saves time but also reduces paperwork and simplifies record keeping.

QuickBooks provides reminders and alerts about upcoming tax deadlines or payments due. These notices help businesses comply with tax regulations and avoid penalties or fines.

In summary, payroll debt management in QuickBooks offers many benefits, such as accurate calculations, separate tracking of debt accounts, integration with electronic payment systems, and timely reminders. Businesses can use these features effectively to ensure their operations run well while maintaining financial stability.

Handling Sales Tax in QuickBooks

Sales tax is essential to any business transaction, and accurately managing sales tax is critical to maintaining compliance with tax regulations. QuickBooks, a popular accounting software, offers several features that help businesses manage sales taxes effectively.

First, QuickBooks allows users to set sales tax rates based on location. This feature ensures that the correct sales tax rate is automatically applied to every transaction.

Users can also create different sales tax codes for their products or services. This flexibility allows businesses to manage complex sales tax situations effectively.

QuickBooks provides tools to track and report sales tax payable. The software generates reports summarizing the amount of sales tax collected during a specific period, making it easier for businesses to file tax returns accurately and promptly. By automating this process, QuickBooks reduces the risk of errors and saves valuable time.

QuickBooks integrates seamlessly with e-commerce platforms and point-of-sale systems. This integration allows businesses to sync their online transactions directly into QuickBooks while automatically applying the appropriate sales tax rates.

Sales tax management in QuickBooks streamlines the process by automating calculations and reporting. This accounting software simplifies compliance with complex tax requirements with a user-friendly interface and comprehensive features. By using these tools effectively, businesses can ensure accurate record-keeping while minimizing errors in their financial reporting.

Chapter Six

Customizing QuickBooks for Specific Industries

QuickBooks for Retail Businesses

In today's fast-paced retail industry, managing finances and keeping track of sales can be daunting. However, with the advent of QuickBooks, retail businesses have found an efficient solution to their accounting needs. QuickBooks is a powerful software that offers a range of features specifically designed for retail businesses.

One of the key benefits of QuickBooks for retail businesses is its ability to track inventory. With this software, retailers can easily monitor stock levels, set reorder points, and generate reports on product performance. This feature helps prevent out-of-stock and allows businesses to make informed decisions about purchasing and pricing.

Another benefit of QuickBooks is its seamless integration with point-of-sale (POS) systems. Retailers can automatically transfer sales data into the software by integrating their point-of-sale system with QuickBooks. This eliminates the need for manual data entry and reduces the risk of errors or discrepancies in financial records.

Additionally, QuickBooks offers powerful reporting capabilities that allow retailers to analyze sales trends, identify best-selling products, and track customer behavior. This information allows businesses to optimize operations and design effective marketing strategies.

In short, QuickBooks has revolutionized financial management for retail businesses. Its inventory tracking features, integration with point-of-sale systems, and comprehensive reporting capabilities make it an indispensable tool in today's competitive market. By effectively leveraging the features of this software, retailers can streamline their accounting processes and gain valuable insights into their business performance.

Tips for Retailers

- If you are a retailer who doesn't want to feel overloaded with recording so many sales receipts, follow these tips to help you record retail sales better.

- When you want to record a sales receipt for an individual deposit you make, you can indicate that a certain sales receipt transaction is deposited once into your bank account. It makes it easy to compare the bank account details to the record of sales you made.

- Separate each cash sale from your credit card sales since credit card sales are handled differently.

- You can use the items assigned as non-inventory sections if you don't want the item list to keep tabs on your inventory. For example, some of them are daily AmEx.

- You can address the QuickBooks point of sale system. It will make it easy to keep tabs on Cash sales easily.

- You can decide not to use items to keep tabs on your inventory. Instead, you can use the non-inventory segment. When you do this, QuickBooks will not track the number of items sold daily.

74

QuickBooks for Service-based Companies

In today's fast-paced business world, effective financial management is essential to the success of any business. QuickBooks has become a powerful tool for service-based businesses to streamline their accounting processes and improve productivity.

One of the biggest benefits of QuickBooks for service businesses is the ability to track time and expenses accurately. With a user-friendly interface, employees can easily record billable hours and expenses, ensuring every minute spent on a project counts.

This feature helps create accurate invoices and provides valuable insights into project profitability.

QuickBooks provides comprehensive reporting capabilities that enable service businesses to analyze their financial data effectively. From profit and loss statements to cash flow reports, businesses can understand their financial situation and make informed decisions accordingly.

QuickBooks integrates seamlessly with other software applications commonly used by service businesses, such as customer relationship management (CRM) systems or project management tools. Another important benefit of using QuickBooks is the ability to automate repetitive tasks.

By setting up recurring invoices or automatic payment reminders, service businesses can save valuable time and significantly reduce administrative burdens.

QuickBooks has become an indispensable tool for service businesses looking to improve their financial management processes. Time tracking features, powerful reporting capabilities, integration options with other software applications, and automation capabilities make it the ideal choice for streamlining operations and improving productivity and capacity in these organizations.

QuickBooks for Nonprofits and Charities

In today's digital age, effective financial management is critical for nonprofit and charitable organizations to fulfill their missions effectively. QuickBooks, a popular accounting software, has emerged as a valuable tool. With a user-friendly interface and powerful features, QuickBooks provides the ideal solution for these organizations to streamline their financial processes.

One of the biggest benefits of QuickBooks is the ability to track donations accurately. Nonprofit organizations rely primarily on donations from individuals and businesses to fund their activities. QuickBooks allows them to record these contributions systematically, ensuring transparency and accountability. In addition, the software also allows users to create detailed reports on income and expenses, making budget planning and financial analysis easier.

Another notable feature of QuickBooks is its ability to manage grants effectively. Many nonprofit organizations receive funding from government agencies or organizations for specific projects or programs. QuickBooks enables organizations to properly allocate capital, monitor spending against funding requirements, and generate reports demonstrating compliance with funding guidelines.

The software simplifies payroll management for nonprofit organizations with employees or volunteers. It automatically calculates taxes, tracks employee hours, quickly generates paychecks or direct deposits, and ensures compliance with labor laws.

In short, QuickBooks has become an indispensable tool for nonprofits and charities looking for effective financial management solutions. The ability to accurately track donations, effectively manage grants, and streamline the payroll process proves valuable in successfully supporting the mission of these organizations. By effectively using this powerful software, nonprofits can focus more on positively impacting their communities instead of being burdened with complex financial tasks.

QuickBooks for Construction and Contracting Businesses

In today's fast-paced business world, effective financial management is essential to the success of any business. This is especially true for construction and contracting companies, where managing multiple projects, tracking costs, and ensuring accurate payments can be difficult. Luckily, QuickBooks offers a comprehensive solution tailored specifically to the needs of these industries. QuickBooks offers many features that help streamline the financial process for construction and contracting companies. A key feature is job costing, which allows businesses to track costs associated with specific projects. This allows for accurate budgeting and helps identify areas where costs can be reduced or managed more effectively.

QuickBooks allows for easy invoicing and payment tracking. Contractors can create professional invoices with detailed information about services and associated costs. The software also enables seamless integration with popular payment platforms, allowing customers to pay bills quickly.

Another advantage of QuickBooks is its ability to create comprehensive reports. Construction companies can access real-time data on project profitability, cash flow analysis, and accounts receivable/payable status. These reports provide valuable information about a company's financial position and help make informed decisions.

QuickBooks simplifies tax preparation by organizing transactions by relevant tax codes. This ensures compliance with tax regulations while minimizing potential errors or omissions when filing.

QuickBooks provides an invaluable set of tools for construction and contracting companies looking for effective financial management solutions. Its job costing capabilities, invoicing features, reporting features, and tax preparation tools make it a key asset for streamlining operations in these industries. By using this software effectively, businesses can improve profits while maintaining accurate financial records.

Chapter Seven
Advanced Features

Managing Inventory and Assemblies

Managing inventory and assembly on QuickBooks is essential to running a successful business. QuickBooks provides a comprehensive platform for tracking and managing inventory, ensuring businesses have accurate inventory levels, costs, and revenue information.

One of the key features of QuickBooks is the ability to track inventory in real-time. This means businesses can easily see how much inventory they have at any given time, allowing them to make informed decisions about purchasing and restocking. Additionally, QuickBooks can generate reports that provide valuable insight into sales trends and inventory turnover rates.

Another important feature of QuickBooks is its ability to handle clusters. An assembly is a product made up of many parts or components. With QuickBooks, businesses can easily create assembly items and track the quantity and cost of each part used in the assembly process. This allows for accurate costing and pricing of assembled products.

Additionally, QuickBooks allows businesses to set reorder points for items in their inventory. Reorder points help businesses never run out of stock by automatically creating orders when inventory drops below a specified threshold.

This feature simplifies the purchasing process and reduces the risk of being out of stock.

In short, inventory and assembly management on QuickBooks is important for businesses that want to optimize their operations. The platform's real-time tracking capabilities, assembly management features, and automated reorder point system allow businesses to manage inventory levels while minimizing costs and maximizing profits effectively.

Tracking Time and Mileage

In today's fast-paced business world, efficient time and expense management is crucial for any organization. QuickBooks, a popular accounting software, offers a comprehensive solution for tracking time and mileage. This feature allows businesses to record employee hours accurately and monitor travel expenses, resulting in better financial control and improved productivity.

One of the key benefits of using QuickBooks for time tracking is its simplicity. The software provides an intuitive interface that enables employees to log their hours worked on specific projects or tasks easily. This information can then be used to generate accurate invoices or payroll reports, saving valuable time for both employees and employers.

Additionally, QuickBooks' mileage tracking feature simplifies the process of recording travel expenses. The software automatically calculates the distance traveled by entering starting and ending locations and applies the appropriate reimbursement rate. This eliminates the need for manual calculations or paper-based logs, reducing errors and ensuring accurate expense reporting.

Furthermore, integrating time and mileage tracking with other financial functions in QuickBooks streamlines overall business operations. Having all the data in one centralized system allows managers to easily analyze project costs, identify inefficiencies, and make informed decisions to optimize resource allocation.

In summary, time and mileage tracking on QuickBooks offers many benefits to businesses looking to manage employee work hours and travel expenses effectively. With a user-friendly interface, automatic calculations, and integration with other finance functions, it improves productivity while providing precise financial control. Adopting this technology is a smart choice for any organization looking to streamline operations in today's competitive market.

Handling Multicurrency Transactions

Handling multicurrency transactions on QuickBooks can be a complex task for businesses operating in the global market. With the rise of globalization, it has become increasingly common for companies to engage in international trade and deal with multiple currencies.

QuickBooks, a popular accounting software, offers various tools and features to simplify this process.

One of the key features of QuickBooks is its ability to handle multicurrency transactions seamlessly. It allows businesses to create invoices, receive payments, and purchase in different currencies. Using the current exchange rate, the software automatically converts foreign currency amounts to the company's base currency.

Users must enable the feature in their settings to enable multi-currency functionality on QuickBooks. Once enabled, they can create accounts in multiple currencies and assign a base currency to each account. This allows for accurately tracking profits or losses due to exchange rate fluctuations.

QuickBooks provides reports that help businesses effectively analyze their multi-currency transactions. These reports include currency transaction reports, realized and unrealized profit/loss reports, and exchange rate lists.

However, businesses must understand that managing multi-currency transactions on QuickBooks requires proper configuration and ongoing maintenance.

Users should regularly update exchange rates to ensure accurate conversions and monitor any potential impact on financial reporting.

QuickBooks provides valuable tools for effectively managing multi-currency transactions.

Businesses can streamline their international operations while maintaining financial records by enabling multi-currency functionality and using various features such as invoicing and reporting capabilities.

Using QuickBooks Add-ons and Integrations

QuickBooks has long been recognized as powerful accounting software that helps businesses manage their finances effectively. However, with the advent of technology and the growing needs of businesses, QuickBooks has evolved to offer add-ons and integrations that enhance its functionality even further.

One of the key benefits of using the QuickBooks add-on is the ability to customize the software to meet specific business requirements. These add-ons provide additional functionality not found in the standard version of QuickBooks. For example, there are add-ons for inventory management, project management, time tracking, and more. By integrating these add-ons into QuickBooks, businesses can streamline operations and improve productivity.

Third-party application integration with QuickBooks enables seamless data transfer between different systems. This eliminates the need for manual data entry or copying of records, reducing errors and saving time. For example, integrating a CRM system with QuickBooks allows businesses to synchronize customer information easily.

Additionally, using add-ons and integrations on QuickBooks provides businesses with real-time insight into their finances. With these tools, businesses can create detailed reports and analytics that help them make informed decisions about their finances.

Using QuickBooks add-ons and integrations brings many benefits to businesses. From customization options to streamlined operations and advanced reporting capabilities, these tools enable organizations to optimize their financial management processes effectively. As technology advances rapidly, businesses must use these innovations to stay competitive in today's dynamic marketplace.

Chapter Eight
Troubleshooting and Tips

Common Errors and How to Fix Them

QuickBooks is a widely used accounting software that helps businesses manage financial transactions effectively. However, like any other software, it is prone to errors that can disrupt your business.

A common error is "Error 3371: Unable to initialize license attribute". This error occurs when QuickBooks fails to load license data because the file is corrupt or missing. Delete the permissions file and re-enter your product information to fix this error.

Another common error is the message "Connection lost." This error often occurs when there are problems with the network or company files. To resolve this issue, check your Internet connection and ensure all users are signed out of QuickBooks before trying to sign in again.

Many users are experiencing issues related to bank feeds not updating in QuickBooks. To resolve this issue, check for any pending updates for your bank account and manually refresh your bank feed.

While using QuickBooks can greatly simplify your accounting work, it's important to know about common errors and how to resolve them quickly. By understanding these errors and following the appropriate resolution steps, you can ensure uninterrupted use of QuickBooks and maintain accurate financial records for your business.

Optimizing QuickBooks Performance

QuickBooks is a widely used accounting software that helps businesses manage financial transactions effectively. However, as the amount of data increases, users may experience reduced performance. Optimizing QuickBooks settings and taking necessary actions is essential to ensure optimal performance.

First, regularly updating QuickBooks to the latest version can significantly improve its performance. Intuit, the company behind QuickBooks, releases updates that fix bugs and improve system stability. These updates also provide new features and improvements that can improve efficiency.

Another important step is regularly cleaning up your company profile by deleting unnecessary data. Over time, outdated or unused information can accumulate and slow down software performance. Deleting or archiving old transactions can help reduce file size and improve speed.

Additionally, optimizing hardware resources is important for optimal performance. Increasing the amount of RAM or using an SSD instead of a traditional hard drive can significantly improve QuickBooks' speed.

Advanced reporting features such as summary reports instead of detailed reports can save processing time. Customizing report options to display only relevant information will also help improve efficiency.

Finally, one should not neglect regular maintenance tasks such as checking data integrity and rebuilding data files. These actions help identify and correct any company file structure errors.

In summary, optimizing QuickBooks performance requires a combination of software updates, cleaning unnecessary data, upgrading hardware resources when necessary, judicious use of advanced reporting features, and running regular maintenance tasks. By diligently following these steps, users can ensure smooth operations with improved efficiency in their financial management process using QuickBooks.

Data Backup and Recovery Strategies

In today's digital age, data backup and recovery strategies have become essential for businesses of all sizes. QuickBooks, the popular accounting software many organizations use, is no exception. Implementing effective backup and recovery strategies is critical to ensuring the security and integrity of financial data stored in QuickBooks.

One of the most popular methods of backing up QuickBooks data is using cloud-based solutions. Cloud storage allows businesses to securely store their data off-site, reducing the risk of damage or physical loss due to natural disasters or theft. Services like Dropbox or Google Drive offer seamless integration with QuickBooks, allowing for automatic backups at regular intervals.

Another strategy is to create a local backup on an external hard drive or network-attached storage (NAS) device. These backups provide an additional layer of security by keeping a copy of the data on-premise. However, it is important to test these backups regularly to ensure they work properly and can be restored when needed. In addition to contingency strategies, it is equally important to have a solid recovery plan. This includes documenting step-by-step procedures for restoring data from backups and assigning responsibilities to specific individuals within the organization. Regular training sessions should also familiarize employees with the recovery process.

In conclusion, implementing effective backup and recovery strategies in QuickBooks is vital for safeguarding financial data. By utilizing cloud-based solutions and creating local backups, businesses can minimize the risk of data loss due to unforeseen circumstances.

Furthermore, having a well-defined recovery plan ensures that potential disruptions can be quickly resolved without significantly impacting operations.

Tips and Tricks for Efficient Bookkeeping

Effective bookkeeping is vital for any business, and QuickBooks has become one of the most popular accounting software solutions. With a user-friendly interface and powerful features, QuickBooks can streamline your accounting process and save you valuable time.

Here are some tips and tricks to help you get the most out of QuickBooks for efficient accounting.

First, it is essential to set up your chart of accounts correctly. This will ensure that all transactions are classified correctly, making it easier to create accurate financial reports. Take the time to customize your chart of accounts to your business's needs.

Second, use bank feeds in QuickBooks. By connecting your bank account directly to QuickBooks, you can automatically import transactions, saving you the hassle of entering each transaction manually. This feature also allows you to reconcile your bank statements quickly.

Third, take advantage of keyboard shortcuts in QuickBooks. Learning these keyboard shortcuts can significantly speed up data entry tasks and software navigation.

Also, regularly reconcile your accounts in QuickBooks. Reconciliation ensures that all transactions are recorded accurately and allows any discrepancies or errors to be quickly identified.

Additionally, use the reports available in QuickBooks to understand your business's finances. Customize these reports to your needs and review them regularly to make better decisions.

In short, following these tips and tricks for efficient accounting in QuickBooks can streamline your accounting process and save valuable time. Use the software's features efficiently and stay organized with accurate financial records.

Chapter Nine
Expanding Your Knowledge

Professionals must continuously expand their knowledge and skills in today's rapidly evolving business world. One area of great importance is QuickBooks, a widely used accounting software. By expanding your knowledge of QuickBooks, you can improve your overall efficiency, accuracy, and productivity.

First, expanding your knowledge of QuickBooks allows you to streamline your financial processes. With a user-friendly interface and comprehensive features, QuickBooks lets you easily manage invoices, track expenses, and create financial reports. By understanding the software's advanced functionalities, such as payroll management or inventory tracking, you can optimize your workflow and save valuable time.

A deep understanding of QuickBooks empowers you to make informed decisions based on accurate financial data. The software provides real-time insights into the financial health of your business through customizable reports and dashboards. By mastering these reporting tools and learning to interpret the data effectively, you can promptly identify trends or areas that need improvement.

Furthermore, expanding your knowledge in QuickBooks opens up new career opportunities. Many businesses need experts to be proficient in using this software for their accounting needs. By becoming a QuickBooks expert, you can differentiate yourself from others in the job market and increase your chances of landing lucrative positions or promotions.

In short, expanding your knowledge of QuickBooks is vital for professionals who want to excel in today's competitive business landscape. It enables streamlined financial processes informed decisions based on accurate data analysis, and opens up new career opportunities. Therefore, investing time and effort to learn more about this powerful accounting software is a wise decision that will benefit those who want to develop their careers.

Advanced Training Resources

QuickBooks is a widely used accounting software that helps businesses manage financial transactions effectively. While it offers a user-friendly interface, mastering QuickBooks' advanced features requires appropriate training and resources. Fortunately, various advanced training resources are available to help users improve their skills and maximize the benefits of this powerful software.

Online courses are a valuable resource for advanced QuickBooks training. Many reputable websites offer comprehensive courses covering advanced reporting, inventory management, payroll processing, and more. These courses are designed to provide in-depth knowledge and practical application of advanced QuickBooks features.

QuickBooks Forum and Community is another useful resource. These online platforms allow users to connect with other experienced users who can offer advice and answer specific questions about complex tasks or troubleshooting problems.

Try. Participating in these forums expands knowledge and fosters a sense of community among QuickBooks users.

Many books and ebooks also delve into the complexities of QuickBooks' advanced features. These resources often include step-by-step instructions, practical examples, and expert advice to help users easily navigate complex accounting processes.

Attending live seminars or webinars led by certified QuickBooks instructors can benefit those looking for hands-on experience with the software's advanced features.

Soft. These interactive sessions provide the opportunity to learn directly from experts while effectively responding to individual queries.

In short, mastering the advanced features of QuickBooks requires access to appropriate training resources. Online courses, forums/communities, books/ebooks, and webinars/workshops contribute to increasing understanding of this powerful accounting software. By utilizing these resources effectively, individuals can proficiently use QuickBooks' advanced functionalities and optimize its capabilities for their business needs.

Certified QuickBooks ProAdvisor Program

The Certified QuickBooks ProAdvisor program is a highly regarded certification program designed to enhance accounting professionals' skills and expertise in using QuickBooks software. This program, brought to you by Intuit, the creators of QuickBooks, provides individuals with comprehensive training and resources to master this popular accounting software.

To become a Certified QuickBooks Consultant, candidates must complete a series of rigorous training modules and pass an exam testing their knowledge of various aspects of QuickBooks. These modules cover setting up company records, managing accounts receivable and payable, processing payroll, managing inventory, and generating financial reports. By earning this certification, accountants can demonstrate proficiency in effectively using QuickBooks for their clients' bookkeeping needs. They have access to exclusive benefits like priority customer support from Intuit, marketing resources to promote their services as a Certified Professional Consultant, and discounts on products QuickBooks products.

Becoming a certified QuickBooks Consultant improves an accountant's credibility and marketability. It assures potential customers that they are working with professionals skilled in managing their financial records accurately and efficiently.

The Certified QuickBooks ProAdvisor program is an invaluable opportunity for accounting professionals to expand their knowledge and expertise using QuickBooks software. By achieving this certification, accountants can improve their career prospects while providing top-notch services to their clients.

Online Communities and Forums for QuickBooks Users

In today's digital age, online communities and forums have become an indispensable part of our lives. They provide a platform for like-minded people to connect, share knowledge, and seek help. One such community that has become widely popular is the online community for QuickBooks users.

QuickBooks, a widely used accounting software, has revolutionized how businesses manage their finances. However, navigating the various features and troubleshooting issues can sometimes be difficult. This is where online communities and forums come to the rescue.

These platforms bring together a diverse group of QuickBooks users willing to share their experiences, tips, and tricks. Whether you're a beginner or an advanced user, these communities provide valuable information on how to use QuickBooks effectively.

These forums act as a support system where users can seek advice from experts or other users facing similar challenges. The collective wisdom of the community ensures that no question goes unanswered.

Online communities also serve as a hub for staying updated with the latest news and updates related to QuickBooks. Users can find information about new features, updates on tax regulations, and even job opportunities in the accounting field.

In conclusion, online communities and forums for QuickBooks users have become indispensable resources for individuals seeking assistance with this powerful accounting software. These platforms foster collaboration among users while providing access to expert advice and up-to-date information. So whether you want to enhance your skills or troubleshoot an issue with QuickBooks, joining these communities will undoubtedly benefit your journey toward financial management excellence.

Conclusion

Glossary of QuickBooks Terms

The QuickBooks Glossary is an essential resource for individuals and businesses using popular accounting software. QuickBooks has become a vital part of the financial management industry, allowing users to streamline their accounting processes and gain valuable insights into the financial health of their business. However, navigating the various features and functions can be tedious without understanding the terminology.

An important term included in the glossary is "chart of accounts." This is a complete list of all the accounts a business uses to record its financial transactions. It classifies these accounts into assets, liabilities, equity, income, and expenses. Understanding this term is crucial for setting up accurate financial reports and tracking business performance effectively.

Another important term is "bank reconciliation". This process involves comparing the transactions recorded in QuickBooks with those on bank statements to ensure they match. Bank reconciliations help identify any discrepancies or errors that may have occurred during recording or banking processes.

Additionally, terms such as "accounts payable" and "accounts receivable" are defined in the glossary. Accounts payable refers to money a company owes suppliers or vendors for goods or services received but not yet paid for. On the other hand, accounts receivable represent money owed to a company by its customers for goods or services provided but not yet paid for.

In conclusion, accessing a comprehensive glossary of QuickBooks terms is vital for anyone utilizing this software. Understanding these terms allows users to navigate through QuickBooks confidently and accurately while managing their finances efficiently.

Keyboard Shortcuts Reference

Keyboard shortcuts are essential tools for efficient navigation and increased productivity in any software application. QuickBooks, the popular accounting software, offers many shortcuts that significantly streamline workflows and save valuable time.

One of QuickBooks's most commonly used keyboard shortcuts is Ctrl + I, which opens the Create Invoice window. This shortcut eliminates the need to navigate multiple menus and allows users to create invoices for their customers quickly. Similarly, Ctrl + E opens the Edit Transactions window, allowing users to change or update existing transactions without searching different menus.

Another useful keyboard shortcut is Ctrl + F, which opens the Find window. This feature lets users quickly search for specific transactions or information in their QuickBooks database. Using this shortcut, accountants can easily locate relevant data without wasting time looking through lists or lengthy reports.

Keyboard shortcuts such as Ctrl + D (Delete), Ctrl + N (New), and Ctrl + S (Save) provide quick access to common QuickBooks functions. These keyboard shortcuts eliminate the need for repetitive clicking and allow users to perform tasks efficiently.

In short, using keyboard shortcuts in QuickBooks is important for maximizing productivity and streamlining workflows. By remembering these shortcuts and incorporating them into daily use, accountants can save valuable time navigating menus and completing routine tasks. The ability to quickly create invoices, edit transactions, search for specific information, and perform common functions helps improve efficiency and ensure accurate financial management in QuickBooks.

Sample Forms and Templates

QuickBooks is a widely used accounting software that offers a variety of features to streamline business operations. One of its main advantages is the availability of forms and templates, which can significantly simplify creating professional-looking documents. One of those forms is an invoice template, which allows businesses to create invoices quickly and effectively. With customizable fields for company information, item descriptions, quantities, and prices, users can easily create invoices that suit their specific needs. This not only saves time but also ensures payment accuracy.

Another useful form is the order form. Businesses can easily create orders for the goods and services they need using this feature. The template includes fields for supplier information, item details, quantity requested, and expected delivery date. This simplifies the procurement process by providing a standardized format that can be easily shared with suppliers.

QuickBooks provides templates for other important documents such as sales receipts, estimates or quotes, credit notes, and purchase orders. These templates allow businesses to maintain consistency in communication with customers and suppliers.

QuickBooks forms and templates significantly benefit businesses by simplifying the document creation process. They save time and effort while ensuring the accuracy and professionalism of various financial transactions. These templates allow a business to focus on its core activities while maintaining effective record-keeping practices.